WALKS F

IN AND AROUI

CW00829725

36 LINEAR WALKS and 49 CIRCULAR ...

PAT TIDSALL AND ROMA WILCOCK

Follow the Countryside code

1) Be safe and plan ahead and follow any signs

2) Keep dogs under control

3) Prevent uncontrolled moorland fires

4) Protect plants and animals, take your litter home

5) Leave gates and property as you find them

6) Consider other people

7) Beware mineshafts! Derbyshire alone has over 100,000 mine shafts. Keep away from depressions in the ground in the mining areas of the Peak District. Several of the walks in this book pass through mining areas, so stay on rights of way at all times.

Published by **Ashbourne Editions**
Unit 3, Peak Business Centre, Moor Farm Road West,
Ashbourne, Derbyshire, DE6 1HD
Tel: (01335) 347349
Fax: (01335) 347303

ISBN: 978-1-873775-41-7

British Library Cataloguing in Publication Data: a catalogue
record for this book is available from the British Library.

Printed by: Gomer Press Ltd

Design & reproduction by: Mark Titterton

Photography: p.56 & p.76 © Mark Titterton

All other photography by the author

Acknowledgements: Pat wishes to thank her husband, Peter, for all his
assistance and encouragement in compiling this book and to Stella Porter, the
publisher, for her patience and attention to detail in the production of this book.

Front cover: View from Ilam Visitor Centre with Thorpe Cloud in the distance
Back cover: Stepping Stones, Dovedale
Opposite page: Chatsworth House

WALKS FOR ALL AGES

IN AND AROUND THE PEAK DISTRICT

36 LINEAR WALKS and 49 CIRCULAR WALKS

PAT TIDSALL AND ROMA WILCOCK

All the walks start at recognised car parks unless stated otherwise in the detailed walk descriptions.

LOCATION MAP & KEY (OPPOSITE)

Above: Footpath to the stepping stones from the car park at Dovedale

~~	All Roads
- - - - - -	Trails
~~	Rivers
⌒	Lakes
CP	Car Parks
BAKEWELL	Area
Monsal Head	Venues

WALK INDEX

AREA & VENUE	LINEAR	DISTANCES	CIRCULAR	DISTANCES	PAGE
ASHBOURNE AREA					
Alstonefield/Milldale	1	3 miles			11
Ashbourne	1	Variable	1	3 miles	12
Dimmingsdale	3	Variable	3	½, to 3 miles	14
Hartington	3	Variable	2	2 ½ & 3 miles	17
		1 & 2 miles			
Ilam and Dovedale	1	Variable	4	¾ to 2 ½ miles	21
Newhaven	1	2½ miles			24
Tissington	1	Variable	3	¾ to 3 miles	25
BAKEWELL AREA					
Ashford-in-the-Water	1	2 miles	1	3 miles	29
Bakewell	2	1¼ miles	2	2 & 3 ½ miles	31
Birchover & Stanton Moor			1	2 miles	34
Lathkill Dale	1	Variable	2	2 & 3 ½ miles	36
Monsal Head & The Longstones			5	1 ½ to 3 ½ miles	39
BASLOW AREA					
Baslow & Curbar	2	1¾ to 3 miles	2	2 & 3 miles	46
Calver	1	Variable	2	3 & 3 ½ miles	50
Chatsworth	3	½ to 1¼ mile	1	4 miles	53
BUXTON AREA					
Buxton	1	Variable			58
Errwood Reservoir	2	Variable	1	3 miles	58
Lud's Church & The Roaches			2	3 & 4 miles	61

6

AREA & VENUE	LINEAR	DISTANCES	CIRCULAR	DISTANCES	PAGE
CASTLETON AREA					
Castleton	1	2 miles	2	1 ½ & 2 ¼ miles	65
Hathersage	2	¾ mile	1	3 miles	67
Hope	1	Variable	2	3 to 3½ miles	69
Longshaw & Grindleford	3	½ to 1½ miles	4	1½ to 3¾ miles	72
MATLOCK AREA					
Black Rocks	2	½ & 1½ miles			79
Cromford	1	1¼ miles	2	¾ & 3 miles	81
Matlock Bath			1	1 mile	84
TIDESWELL AREA					
Eyam			3	2 & 4 miles	86
Tideswell	2	2 miles	2	3 & 4miles	90
Please note all linear walks are as far as you wish – described here as "Variable" – the distances stated above are only for those walks where there is a pick up point.					
OTHER OUTINGS					
Barton Turns Marina					93
Carsington Reservoir					93
Elvaston Park					93
Melbourne Hall					94
National Memorial Arboretum					94
Rudyard Lake					95
Staunton Harold					95
Tittesworth Reservoir					96

Note: The Majority of linear walks are suitable for wheelchair users, at their own discretion.

INTRODUCTION

One of the most wonderful aspects of our lives is the enjoyment of our glorious and beautiful countryside.

This book is an attempt to enable young families and those of us whose mobility has been limited by age illness or accident to share in that enjoyment. It will also bring about the chance of visiting previously unknown areas of our region as well as those much loved and remembered.

Derbyshire is well blessed with the routes of old mineral railway lines. These have been converted into trails:- The Monsal, Tissington and High Peak (now called the Pennine Way). These trail surfaces are mostly level and made of compacted stone and shale. They provide relatively easy conditions for all uses at your own discretion.

THIS IS THE WAY THE BOOK WORKS

The Tissington Trail can be accessed from:- Ashbourne, Thorpe, Tissington Alsop, Alsop Moor (layby), Hartington Station and Parsley Hay where the High Peak and Tissington Trails meet.

The High Peak Trail can be accessed from:- High Peak Junction, Black Rocks, Middleton Top, Minninglow, Friden and Sparklow.

The Monsal Trail can be accessed from:- Bakewell, Hassop Station, Thornbridge Hall, Monsal Head, Millers Dale and Topley Pike. The tunnels along the Monsal trail are to be opened in 2011.

1. Each area comprises a number of venues giving a choice of the types of walks possible. A map for each area gives the route to the venues; the scales vary according to the spread of the area covered. There are very few flat walks in Derbyshire except most of the linear walks mentioned in (b) below. Full details for each area and venue are given as follows:-

a) Very short circular walks of ½ to 4 miles. The squeeze and wall stiles can vary from easy to quite difficult. Please note the directions given on the routes are as you stand with your back to the stile/gate.

b) Linear Walks "As far as you wish" and at your own discretion. These walks along trails, woodland tracks and moorlands offer an opportunity for the less agile amongst us to enjoy the countryside. The trails are mainly flat and of hard packed shale. The views are often quite different on the return walk.

c) Pick up points along or at the end of a linear walk are indicated together with the distance from the start.

d) Free parking facilities for "Blue Badge" holders are given. Most of the car parks are "pay and display".

e) Toilets and facilities are indicated – some [mainly public ones for the disabled] need a Radar Key.

f) Refreshment outlets and any places of interest are noted with opening times where known, though these can and do change.

2. We would suggest taking medical advice where relevant and also not being over ambitious! Please wear stout shoes and warm/water proof clothing – the weather can change very quickly on Derbyshire hills and be unforgiving! Walking sticks are a great aid to balance.

3. There are a number of walks with steep climbs for those who like a challenge. We suggest that you read the whole of the walk before setting out so as to be sure that it is suitable for you.

4. You will find the "You're Welcome. A guide to the Peak District for new and infrequent visitors" very helpful. It is available from Information and Visitor Centres.

5. The Peak District and Derbyshire Travel Map or The Touring Map 4 Peak District will help in locating the major towns and villages. For more detail the 1:25000 White Peak, Dark Peak and OS259 are very useful as they show field boundaries, paths, bridleways and trails.

Please note:- The countryside is not static and changes may have taken place between the research for these walks and their publication. For example field boundaries, gates and gateways, diversions round farmyards, signs and waymarks, stiles, signposts and paths may have altered, as well as the uses of land.

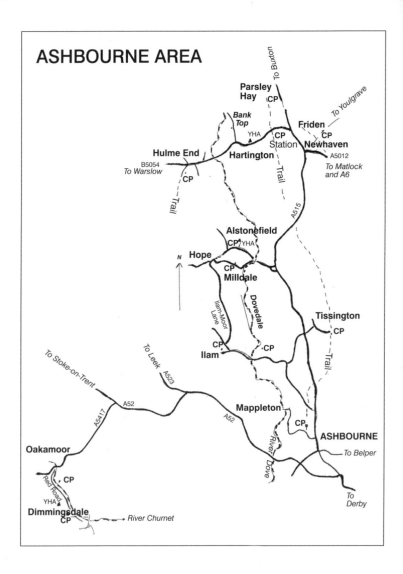

ASHBOURNE AREA

ASHBOURNE AREA

ALSTONEFIELD / MILLDALE

Directions

From Ashbourne take the A515 Buxton Road. In 5 ½ miles turn left to Alstonefield. Follow the minor road for nearly 3 miles crossing the River Dove and climbing up into Alstonefield.

Description

Alstonefield is a pretty village with a well known and frequently visited inn "The George" open daily except Christmas Day. The River Dove, forming the boundary between the Derbyshire and Staffordshire Peak District, is in one of the most beautiful dales in the area.

Milldale Linear 3 miles

Directions to Milldale Car Park. From the entrance to Alstonefield keep straight on passing The George off to the left and at the second parking sign turn left signed "Wetton Ilam Dovedale", in a few metres at a T-junction turn right then left signed "Watts Russell Pub Free Car Park". At the bottom of the hill in Hope the road goes round a left bend to pass the Watts Russell. In about 1 mile after Hope turn into the car park. If you want disabled parking continue down to the hamlet of Milldale where there is parking for 2 cars and a disabled toilet using your radar key.

The small hamlet of Milldale has a kiosk; "Polly's Cottage" providing snacks. The benches on the river bank are places to rest while watching the ducks which are very friendly! This is a very beautiful walk down Dovedale to Dovedale Car Park. Most of the route is along well used paths with gates and stiles but the section of the stepped path over Lover's Leap is rather steep on ascent and descent.

Directions to Dovedale Car Park. Drive back from Milldale to Hope and just past the Watts Russell turn sharp left uphill and almost immediately sharp left again, this is rather a tight turn. Follow the minor road; Stanshope Lane, which goes round a right-hand bend in Stanshope, and then becomes Ilam-Moor Lane. After 3 miles at Ilam you join the main village road by the entrance to Ilam Hall. Drive through Ilam and at the Memorial turn left. In ¾ mile turn left along the minor road to Dovedale Car Park passing the driveway to the Izaak Walton Hotel. [For details of the car park and the hotel see page 23 "Ilam and Dovedale" venue].

Route Instructions

1. From the car park at Milldale walk down to the river and turn right to cross the packhorse bridge then follow the riverside path with gates and stiles.
2. Walk as far as you wish or 3 miles to Dovedale Car Park.

ASHBOURNE

Directions

From the centre of Ashbourne drive up past the open market on the A515 to turn immediately left across the top of the market to follow the signs "Tissington Trail Cycle Hire Centre." In a few metres the road bears round to the right up Dovehouse Green. At the top of the hill keep straight on following the Tissington Trail sign. The car park is on the right a few metres down Mappleton Lane. Grid Ref SK 175470

At the car park as well as cycle hire there is a picnic area, free disabled parking and toilets with a radar key; the main ladies toilets do have hand rails. In the summer there is a small kiosk serving drinks and snacks. A scooter can be hired but you would need to telephone beforehand. ☎ 01335 343156

Description

Ashbourne is the gateway to Dovedale. It is famous for its Royal Shrovetide Football game played on Shrove Tuesday and Ash Wednesday. A game which sets those born on the north side of the River Henmore against those on the south side. The game was given its royal title after the Prince of Wales, turned the ball up, in 1928.

The church of St Oswald is regarded as one of the best sights in Derbyshire having a spire of 212 feet.

Bonnie Prince Charlie declared his father James, King of England, Wales and Scotland when he camped in Ashbourne in December 1745. A plaque in the Market Place commemorates this event.

Ashbourne is rather hilly and parts of it not easy for wheelchairs. The Okeover Arms in Mappleton has a large flat car park and easy access. To reach the inn continue past the entrance to the Tissington Trail car park and in about 1 mile turn right into the car park.

Tissington Trail Linear

From the car park walk to the cycle hire buildings then on along the trail. After about 5 to 10 minutes walking there is a short steep descent and ascent which we are told can be negotiated on a scooter but would need a strong young person to push a wheelchair! The surface is hard packed limestone and flat except for the above.

Tissington Trail and Callow Top Farm
Circular 3 miles

A 1 ½ mile trail walk followed by an undulating route across fields with stiles and gates to Callow Farm where a track and path leads back to the trail.

Route Instructions

1. From the car park walk to the start of the trail by the cycle hire buildings.
2. Follow the Tissington Trail for 1 ½ miles, with the one descent and ascent and crossing over a road.
3. At a crossing of paths turn left off the trail by a footpath sign. Go through a gate.
4. Follow a hedge on the left up the field to cross a fence stile. Aim up the next field to the right-hand end of the buildings. Cross another fence stile.
5. Turn left along the road for a few metres then turn right at the waymarked sign to walk up a wide drive keeping close to the fence and walking between the houses. Cross the stile ahead.
6. Bear left across the open area behind the large farmhouse. This area is being developed so please follow the waymarked signs to cross a fence stile.
7. Bear right across the field ahead to cross a stile in the field corner. Turn right and as you near the field corner bear off left towards the wood, the waymarked stile and large gap.
8. Do NOT cross the stile but turn left to veer away from the wood on the right and aiming for a single tree. Cross a stile in the hedge ahead.
9. Keep straight on to cross another stile then follow the hedge on the left. Cross a stile in the field corner.
10. Continue in the same direction crossing 4 fields, 1 gate and 3 stiles.
11. Follow the field boundary on the left across the next 2 fields aiming for the caravan buildings ahead and crossing 2 stiles. Join the caravan approach road.
12. Turn left down the road. In about 300 metres and opposite the second farm drive on the left turn right over a stile.

13. Almost immediately turn left by the field boundary. Soon you will see the trail down on the left as you walk round the hillside then down towards the trail.
14. Cross a stile and then up steps to the trail.
15. Turn right to retrace your outward route back to the car park.

The Tunnel

If you wish to leave the car at the Tissington Trail Car Park then you can walk into Ashbourne through the lighted tunnel. It will take you about 10 minutes. When you reach the gate into the station car park at the end of the tunnel turn left up a tarmac path to the road. Turn left along the road and then turn right at the T-junction. Walk down Church Street to the centre of the town. To walk there and back will add about 1 mile to your walk.

DIMMINGS DALE

Directions

From Ashbourne take the A52 Leek road. In 4 ½ miles from the western end of the Ashbourne by-pass turn left still on the A52 and leaving the A523 Leek road. In just over 2 ½ miles turn left onto the B5417 Oakamoor road. Follow this road for 2 ¾ miles keeping straight on at a crossroads to follow the Cheadle road, still on the B5417. In Oakamoor cross the river bridge over the Churnet and almost immediately turn left along a minor road signed "Ramblers Retreat". In just over ¼ mile, and having ignored the "station" car park sign, turn left again along Red Road signed "Ramblers Retreat". In about 1 mile turn right into the large free car park by the "Ramblers Retreat." There are no toilet facilities at the car park. Grid Ref SK063431

Description

This is a lovely walking area through the ever changing woodlands of Dimmings Dale. For most of the routes you are on good wide woodland tracks. This area is said to have some of the best autumn walks in the Midlands. The Ramblers Retreat offers snacks, teas, and full meals. For parties you would need to book ☎ 01538 702730. Open every day except over the Christmas period and occasionally in the winter. They are able to offer disabled facilities in the restaurant and a disabled toilet.

Forestry Track 1 Linear

A walk along a wide hard packed forestry track to Earls Rock, which is ½ mile. There is a slight ascent and descent. There is no pick up point.

Route Instructions

From the car park return to the road then immediately turn left at the footpath sign "Smeltingmill Earls Rock".

Forestry Track 2 Linear

An easy walk along the wide, hard packed forestry trail, not as even as track 1 above. There are a number of seats along the first part of the track. It is nearly 1 mile to the picnic area. There is no pick up point.

Route Instructions

1. From the car park walk in front of the Ramblers Retreat. Take the left-hand route passing close to the fence round the garden and outdoor eating area of the Retreat. Follow the wide track passing by the Forestry Commission Boom.
2. Keep the lake and stream on the right.
3. In about ¾ mile and immediately after a wide uphill track on the left, turn right down a short hill.
4. Cross between the two lakes to the picnic site.
5. Retrace your steps back to the car park.

Smeltingmill Circular ½ mile

This walk is along forestry tracks and a narrow rocky path.

Route Instructions

1. From the car park walk in front of the Ramblers Retreat. Take the left-hand route passing close to the fence round the garden and outdoor eating area of the Retreat. Follow the wide track passing by the Forestry Commission Boom.
2. In about 300 metres from the car park and just past a cottage behind the wall on the right and by an old tree stump, turn right.
3. Walk along a short pretty stony path by the lake.
4. At the junction with the wide woodland track turn right.
5. Walk back to the car park.

Oldfurnace Circular 3 miles

This walk follows wide flat forestry tracks, uneven paths, a driveway and a minor road. The latter is quite a steep climb of nearly ½ mile. It is a lovely walk.

Route Instructions

1. From the car park walk in front of the Ramblers Retreat. Take the left-hand route passing close to the fence round the garden and outdoor eating area of the Retreat. Follow the wide track passing by the Forestry Commission Boom.

2. Keep the lake and stream on the right. After about ¾ mile and immediately after a wide uphill track on the left turn right down a short hill.

3. Cross between the two lakes to the picnic site. When you reach the second lake, turn right along a path which separates the two parts of the lake.

4. Turn left, the upper lake is now on the left. Follow the Staffordshire Moorlands Walk for just over ¾ mile. You will pass a boom, cross the stream, pass a lake on the right, then "Old Furnace Cottage" on the left and lastly another stream before you reach the road at Oldfurnace.

5. Turn right to walk up the rather steep minor twisting road [Stoney Dale]. In about ¼ mile turn right to walk up a tarmac drive. Follow the drive, which is part of the Staffordshire Way, for ½ mile. At a fork in the road walk to the Y.H.A. sign.

6. Cross the cattle grid and turn left down the narrow path through the open woodland of Ousal Dale. At a crossing of paths take the right-hand fork [do not turn right] down the narrower path. It is quite stony in places. In nearly ½ mile you will come to Earl's Rock House.

7. Continue ahead with the lake on your right.

After another ¼ mile you will arrive back at the car park ready for a welcome cup of tea!

Dimmings Dale Circular 1 ½ miles

It is advisable to follow this pretty, short woodland route after a very dry period as parts of it can be extremely muddy.

Route Instructions

1. From the car park walk in front of the Ramblers Retreat. Take the left-hand route passing close to the fence round the garden and outdoor eating area of the Retreat. Follow the wide track passing by the Forestry Commission Boom.

2. Keep the lake and stream on the right.

3. Immediately after a wide uphill track on the left turn right down a short hill.
4. Cross between the two lakes to the picnic site and turn right to walk along a narrow path with the stream on your right.
5. Pass a footbridge on the right to continue along the undulating woodland path.
6. On reaching a second footbridge on the right cross it [this can be very muddy].
7. Turn left to follow the partly walled path to Earls Rock where you turn right back to the car park.

Churnet Valley Linear

Directions to Station Car Park at Oakamoor

Follow directions to Oakamoor on page 14. In Oakamoor cross the river bridge over the Churnet and almost immediately turn left along a minor road signed "Ramblers Retreat". In about 150 metres turn left into the Station Car Park. Grid Ref SK 053446

This is a trail along the dismantled railway [as far as you wish with pushchairs and wheelchairs.] It is just over a mile to the Ramblers Retreat but the exit off the trail is either up steps or, after passing under the bridge, a short rather rough forest track to take you across Lord's Bridge to the Retreat.

HARTINGTON

Directions

From Ashbourne take the A515 and in about 11 miles and having passed the Newhaven turn left. Follow the B5054 for nearly 2 ½ miles to Hartington. There are two car parks, one in the centre of the village near the duck pond and a pay and display car park, with disabled free parking, on the right off the B5054 as you drive out of the village towards Warslow. Grid Ref. SK 127603

Description

Hartington is a very lively village and often quite crowded on bank and school holidays. Disabled toilets can be found on the right as you leave the main car park. The village has much to offer including "POTS" a ceramic workshop, "Hart of the Country", "The Old Cheese Shop" with a ramp at the entrance, "Dauphin Antiques", The Beresford Tea Rooms and Post Office and General stores. The Devonshire Arms and The Charles Cotton Hotel provide refreshments. There are no disabled toilets at these venues but the access to the toilets at The Charles Cotton Hotel is easy.

Bank Top Farm Linear 1 mile

A walk from the village along a mainly flat tarmac surface. There is a cattle grid which you can bypass via a gate and a metre of grass. Farmhouse teas are served at the farm, and toilet facilities are available. ☎ 01298 84205/84859 to make sure the owner is at home. This is also a pickup point.

Route Instructions

From the centre of the village take the "Pilsbury 2 ½" route to walk along Dig Street, then up a very gentle climb to Bank Top Farm.

YHA Circular 2 ½ miles

Directions to the start of the walk

From the centre of the village drive back along the B5054 to pass the Beresford Tea Rooms and the Post Office. Just before the telephone kiosk and by the brown YHA sign on the left, turn right up Hall Bank.

In 200 metres park either on the road, or in the YHA car park if you intend to visit their café. Grid Ref SK132606

This route follows tracks and a minor road. One short section of track is very uneven.

Route Instructions

1. About 100 metres past the youth hostel turn right signed "Biggin" onto the cycle route 54.
2. Follow this shale walled track for ¾ mile [20 minutes]. Ignore paths off and just after a track on the left turn right.
3. Follow this walled, shale, stone and grass track for just under ½ mile. [could be difficult for pushchairs!] At a junction of tracks turn right to walk to a tarmac lane.
4. Ignore the Wolfscote Grange route to keep straight on along the minor road [Reynards Lane].
5. Ignore all side tracks and paths. In about 15 minutes you will reach the road junction.
6. Turn right back to the youth hostel or left into Hartington.

Manifold Way Linear

Directions to the Manifold Way Car Park

From Hartington drive along the B5054 Warslow road for about 2 miles. Drive through Hulme End and immediately turn left into the Visitor Centre and Manifold Way Car Park. Grid Ref SK592104 there is disabled free parking.

There are disabled and baby minder facilities open 9.00am to 6.00pm every day, also a café with limited opening in the winter and summer opening 10.00 am to 5.00pm at the Visitor Centre. There is a picnic area.

Route Instructions

From the car park you can walk as far as you wish, then return to the start. The surface is mainly tarmac at the start.

Hartington Station Linear 2 miles

Directions to Hartington Station Car Park

From Hartington drive back along the B5054 towards the A515. In 1 ½ miles and immediately after going under the bridge turn sharp right up the minor road to Hartington Station Car Park, where there is free disabled parking. Grid Ref SK150610

There are disabled and baby minder facilities, refreshment kiosk [closed during the winter] and a picnic area.

Route Instructions

The Tissington Trail is hard packed shale mostly flat. You can take a southerly route or the northerly route towards Parsley Hay.

At Parsley Hay there are disabled facilities and a refreshment kiosk. Open: weekends in winter and 11am-4pm daily in the summer.

To reach Parsley Hay by car from Hartington drive up to the A515 and turn left. In 1 ½ miles turn left and immediately right to the car park. Grid Ref SK146637

Beresford Dale from Hartington Circular 3 miles

This route crosses fields and stiles then along the beautiful Beresford Dale before following undulating field paths back to Hartington.

Route Instructions

1. With the Charles Cotton Hotel on your right walk up the B5054 Warslow road for a few metres and just before "POTS" [the ceramics works and shop on the left,] turn right at the end of a wall in front of a row of stone houses.

2. Continue along a very narrow path between the buildings, walls and fencing going through a squeeze stile and two gates, then between a fence and a wall. Continue to follow a paddock wall close on the left to cross another stile in the paddock corner.

3. Keep straight on across the next five fields and stiles maintaining a south-westerly direction. In the fourth and fifth fields aim for a cottage and the road.

4. After the fifth stile walk to the B5054 and turn right. Walk up the road [Mill Lane] for about 500 metres, passing into Staffordshire. Pass Raikes Farm on the right and the drive to Lower Hurst Farm on the left.

5. Just past the "Little Raikes Footpath" sign and the cottage on the left, turn left at the footpath sign. Cross the stile and descend the field keeping a wall and fence on the left.

6. Go through a small gate and across a footbridge to walk straight on up the next field. Go through a small gate.

7. Keep straight on to Lower Hurst Farm.

8. Cross a stile and follow the fence close on the right below the farm. Cross two more stiles and a small paddock to go through a squeeze stile.

9. Turn left to cross a cattle grid then turn right to follow the wood close on the right.

10. Go through three small gates then over a small footbridge and a stile.

11. Keep straight on across a field of reeds; soon you will have a wood on the left. Cross another footbridge and stile.

12. Keep straight on to go through a gate and stile to reach Beresford Lane.

13. Turn left down the lane, for nearly ½ mile, to the river. Ignore a track off right and pass Beresford House gate.

14. At the river turn left to walk along the beautiful Beresford Dale keeping the river on your right. Cross the footbridge and follow a path which soon climbs up away from the river. Go through a gated stile.

15. Walk up the hill, bearing very slightly right. Pass three waymarked posts then turn down left towards a gate/gateway passing another waymarked post. Go through the gateway and keep straight on to go through another gateway.

16. Turn right uphill then left by another waymarked post. Cross a track via two gates.

17. Follow a shale path with the wall then houses on the left to go through a gate and down steps by the toilets to reach the road into Hartington. Turn right to the village centre or left to the car park.

ILAM AND DOVEDALE

Directions

From Ashbourne take the A515 Buxton road. After about 1 mile turn left to Dovedale. After another 2 miles at the Dog and Partridge in Thorpe follow the road round to the left. Continue along the road driving through Thorpe village. After crossing the cattle grid the view is magnificent and is worthy of a short stop at a small layby if convenient. Drive down the hill and after crossing the bridge over the River Dove follow the road for a further ¾ mile into Ilam. At the monument turn right. Keep straight on following the route to the hall and car park. Grid Ref. SK 131506. It is free parking for National Trust members and disabled. The large notice board gives full details of all disabled facilities as well as a map of the walks.

Description

Ilam is a delightful village where many of the houses are modelled on the Swiss style. The Hall and Visitor Centre serve hot drinks during winter weekends. A small gallery, shop, toilets + disabled and child minder facilities, are all reached from the car park along hard surfaced slabbed paths. The Tea Room is beyond the National Trust shop and is reached via a narrow path and steps. The Tea Room is open: Mar-Jun and Sep/Oct, Mon, Tue and weekends; Jul and Aug, daily. In the summer there is often an ice-cream van just past the monument. The path to the church is flat and hard surfaced. There are a number of seats where you can admire the gardens and the wonderful views across to Thorpe Cloud and Dovedale.

Paradise Walk Circular 1mile

To reach the riverside path you will cross a short grassy and stepped area. The route then follows a good track near the river before climbing a track and crossing a field. There are no stiles.

Route Instructions

1. From the car park take the Visitor Centre route but in a few metres keep straight on through the two arches of the hall passing the YHA.
2. Turn right in front of the hall to cross the grass area and down the steps to the river.
3. Turn right to follow the flat riverside path passing the Battle Stone.
4. In ½ mile go through a small gate by the farmgate.
5. Turn sharp right back on yourself to walk up a track.
6. In about 150 metres bear off slightly right up to the waymarked post where you turn left.
7. Contour the hillside. Soon you will see the car park over to the left. As the hall comes into view the grass track becomes more obvious.
8. Walk to and through a metalled gate.
9. Turn left to the car park or right to the Visitor Centre

Woodland Walk Circular ¾ mile

This lovely walk takes you through the woods along a hard surfaced stepped path. [109steps]

Route Instructions

1. From the car park take the Visitor Centre route but in a few metres keep straight on through the two arches of the hall passing the YHA.
2. Turn right in front of the hall to cross the grass area and down the steps to the river.
3. At the river turn left to and across the humpback bridge.
4. Turn right to follow the river on your right along a flat hard surfaced path.
5. Climb the 98 fairly shallow stone steps before descending via steps and slopes [there are another 11 uphill steps] to the valley.
6. Cross the wooden footbridge to go through a gate, across the field and over the stile.
7. Turn right along the wide track to the field you crossed in instruction 1 and

retrace your outward route.

As an alternative at instruction 7 you can turn left to pick up instruction 3 of the Paradise Walk A. This will give you a walk of 1 ¼ miles.

Manifold Circular 2 ½ miles

A relatively easy route along Paradise Walk and on along the Manifold Valley then return via the undulating Lodge Lane to Ilam Village.

Route Instructions

1. Leave the car park via the National Trust sign to the Visitor Centre. Continue past the shop and Tea Rooms to follow the winding and partly stepped path down to the Manifold River.

2. Turn right to follow the riverside path keeping the meandering River Manifold over to your left. Notice the Battle Stone on the right. After about ½ mile go through a small gate by the farmgate.

3. Continue ahead, still following the river, to cross a metal stile then three small gates to reach a minor road.

4. Turn right to follow Lodge Lane for about ¾ mile. The lane starts with a climb. When you reach the village bear round to the right to follow the path to the church then on up to the car park.

Dovedale Linear or Circular 2 miles

Directions to the Izaak Walton Hotel and Dovedale Car Park

From Ilam National Trust Car Park drive back through the village passing the monument on your right. In about ¾ mile turn left up a minor road. The Izaak Walton driveway is immediately off to the left. For the Dovedale Car Park continue along the road for nearly ½ mile. [Parking £2 no concessions]. There are disabled toilets [key needed] and a "barn" serving snacks and also National Trust information. Open: daily Apr-Nov and weekends in the winter.

An easy walk along a tarmac drive to the stepping stones. Return walk to the car park as there is no pick up point. The stones have recently been restored to minimise the likelihood of them being flooded.

The Izaak Walton Hotel has a cosy lounge for light meals and an extensive garden eating area with easy access. It also has disabled facilities.

Route Instructions

1. From the car park walk past the toilets to follow the flat tarmac drive to the stepping stones.

2. When the river is low you can cross the stones and turn left by the seat to go through the stile.

3. Follow the well used clear path up the dale for as far as you wish.

4. There is quite a steep stepped climb up over Lover's Leap. This is an interesting rock outcrop for a picnic stop before returning to the car park.

For the circular route cross the stepping stones and turn right to follow the narrow scree and rocky path; sometimes almost in the water! Cross the footbridge over the river and turn left back to the car park.

NEWHAVEN

Friden and High Peak Trail [Pennine Bridleway] Linear 2 ½ miles

A there and back walk as far as you wish on a fairly flat hard packed limestone surface.

From Ashbourne take the A515 north and in about 10 miles at Newhaven turn right, just before a garage, on to the A5012. In a few metres pass Carriages Restaurant to turn left. Drive up the road for about ¼ mile then turn right up to the Friden Car Park. It is a large flat parking area with picnic tables. The short grass and packed limestone path [50 metres] takes you to the trail.

You can walk north-west to Parsley Hay [2 ½ miles], south-west to Minninglow Car Park [2 ½ miles] or there and back as far as you wish. Some parts of the route are not as good as others and this may decide how far you go!

After your walk Carriages Restaurant [Italian] is available to have either a bar snack or a full meal. Opening times: Wed-Sat 12-2pm and 6.30-9.30pm, Sunday 12–1pm. They have a large car park, a flat entrance and bar area and some assistance in the toilets. ☎ 01298 84528 E: carriages.restaurant@tiscali.co.uk

TISSINGTON

Directions

From Ashbourne take the A515 Buxton road, in 4 miles turn right down The Avenue. Keep straight on through the village to turn right down to the Tissington Trail pay and display Car Park. Grid Ref, SK178521 The large flat car park has toilet facilities [plus disabled] also a refreshment kiosk serving light snacks and drinks. Opening: 11am–4pm weekdays and 10.30am–5pm weekends from Mar to Oct. The picnic area is to the south of the car park.

Description

This venue gives you a range of interests.

Tissington Hall is open to visitors at set times; for more details ☎ 01335 352200

The well dressings start on Ascension Day in May for 1 week. The church is also well worth a visit.

The Old Coach House serves coffee, lunch, and afternoon tea opening every day from 10.30am-5pm; Mar to Oct; and Nov to Feb, Thu to Sun [weather permitting]. It has disabled facilities.

In the village there are The Acanthus gift shop [a real Aladdin's cave!], a butchery, a nursery, a candle workshop and glass studio [☎ 0796223244].

Spring is a good time to visit this delightful village when the spring flowers are in bloom.

The Tissington Trail Linear

A trail walk as far as you wish either north or south. The trail surface is of compacted shale. Wheelchair users should use their own discretion as to the suitability of the trail for them. We have talked to wheelchair users on the trail and they have found it suitable.

After the walk you can drive into the village to park where indicated.

The Trail Circular ¾ mile

A trail with steps and fields with a stile and gates,

Route Instructions

1. With your back to the pay machine head towards and under the bridge to follow the trail.

2. In about 15 to 20 minutes at a crossing of paths turn left up 19 steps to go through a stepped squeeze stile, with about a three foot drop to the field.

3. Keep straight on across the field to go through a gated squeeze stile. Continue ahead to go through another gated squeeze stile by a farmgate/gateway.

Bear left across the third field to go through a small gate. Walk down to the surfaced drive and turn right.

4. At the T-junction by the butchers shop turn left. Follow the village road up to the next road junction and turn left. Almost immediately turn right back to the car park.

The Tissington Trail

Trail and Village Circular 1 ½ miles

A walk along the trail then a short narrow path with 6 steps to a minor undulating road.

Route Instructions

1. Follow the trail for about ¾ of a mile; there is a seat, with wonderful views, along the way

2. Just before you reach the second bridge turn left up 6 steps to walk up a narrow path for 100 metres. Go through a small gate and turn left.

3. Follow the undulating minor road [Flatts Lane] for just over ¼ mile.

4. Turn left down Chapel Lane then on into the village down The Foot passing the Butchers shop.

5. Walk up to the road junction and turn left back to the car park.

The Village and Rakes Lane Circular 3 miles

An easy walk along village roads, fields with stiles and the trail.

Route Instructions

1. Leave the car park via the main entrance. Turn left back into the village. Pass the duck pond on your left then turn right to walk up the main road through the village passing The Coach House Tea Rooms and Tissington Hall.

2. Keep straight on up and out of the village ignoring all side roads and paths. In about 150 metres, where the road bends left up Rakes Lane keep straight on.

3. Follow the walled track to cross a stile by a farmgate. Keep the wall on the left across the field passing a copse of trees on the right. Cross another stile by a farmgate. You now have a copse on your left and a wall.

4. In the top left-hand corner of the field enter a walled track for a few metres, before continuing in the same direction to enter another short walled track. At the end of this section of track bears right across and down the field aiming for a farmgate.

5. Cross the stile onto the Tissington Trail and turn right.

6. Follow the trail for 1 ½ miles, back to the car park.

BAKEWELL AREA

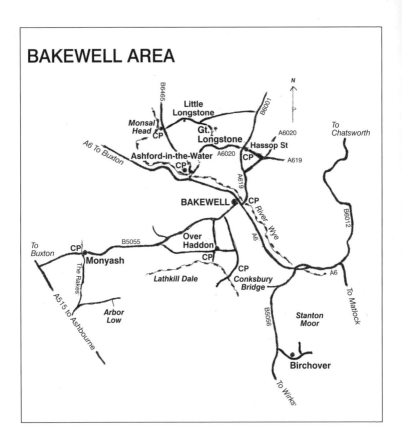

BAKEWELL AREA

ASHFORD-IN-THE-WATER

Directions

From Bakewell take the A6 Buxton road. In 1 ½ miles turn right at the A6020 Chesterfield and Sheffield sign and in a few metres turn left into Ashford village. Ignore the B6465 to Monsal Head and keep straight on through the village, passing the church on the right. At the end of the road turn right up Fennel Street. Near the top of the street turn right to follow the car parking signs. Grid Ref, SK 195697. It is a free car park with toilets + disabled toilets with the radar key.

Description

Ashford-in-the-Water is a delightful village. It is famous for the Sheep Wash Bridge at the bottom of Fennal Street. In mediaeval times it was a packhorse bridge but it is best known for sheep washing. The lambs would be kept within the stone-walled pen on one side of the river whilst the sheep were thrown in at the other side. The sheep would then swim across to their lambs thus having a good "bath!"

On the Saturday before Trinity Sunday in May five or six wells are dressed. Many people visit the well dressings during the week.

The church is well worth a visit. There you will see funeral garlands, the oldest dating back to the 18th Century.

The Aisseford Tea Rooms [no fully disabled facilities], the Bulls Head [with disabled parking and toilets radar key] and the Ashford Arms [with disabled parking and toilets] all offer refreshments.

Monsal Trail & Churchdale Hall Circular 3 miles

A relatively easy walk across fields with stiles, the trail, a driveway and a short road stretch.

Route Instructions

1. From the car park return to Fennel Street and turn right up Vicarage Lane. Pass the entrance to Highfields and just past the decontrolled sign turn right through a stile to cross a small field and then through a gated stile.
2. Cross the road to go down a walled track and over a walled stile. Walk up the

field ahead keeping a wall close on the right. Go through a gate. Continue in the same direction with the wall on the right. Cross the stile in the field corner.

3. Cross Longstone Lane to go through a stile.

4. Walk up the field and through a gated stile. Continue in the same direction crossing three fields and stiles. In the fourth field aim for the rail and steps ahead which take you up onto the Monsal Trail.

5. Turn right along the Monsal Trail for about ¾ mile passing Thornbridge Hall and the old station. You will pass under three bridges before crossing over a road bridge, at which point turn left down a narrow path to the road.

6. Turn left down to a T-junction then walk under the bridge. In a few metres at the next road junction follow the Ashford sign by the grass triangle. Cross the busy A6020 to walk up the drive signed "Private No Parking" and "Public Footpath".

7. Follow the drive for nearly ½ mile passing Churchdale Farm and the entrance to Churchdale Hall. Stay on the main drive going through the gate/gateway. A few metres further on leave the drive to cross a stile.

8. Continue ahead following the boundary wall and ha-ha of the hall over to the right. Cross the wall stile by a stand of trees.

9. Walk down the middle of the next two fields crossing two fence stiles before entering a wood. Follow the path downhill through the trees to go through a gate and a squeeze stile to the main road.

10. Turn left along the A6020 [it is advisable to use the pavement on the right-hand side of the road]. As you approach Ashford stay on the pavement to cross a small stile on the right, by the footpath post and just before the first house, on the right.

11. Walk down the fenced and walled path to go through a stile onto the driveway. Turn right into the village. At the T-junction turn left then right by The Ashford Arms. Follow Church Street passing The Bulls Head and the church to walk to the octagonal memorial shelter.

12. Turn right up Fennel Street back to the car park.

Monsal Dale View and Monsal Head Linear 2 miles

From Ashford to the seat above Monsal Dale is about 1 ½ miles along tracks and up a field. There is no pick up point but the view is wonderful. Another ½ mile down a narrow rocky path will bring you to Monsal Head where there is a pick up point and refreshments.

Route Instructions

1. From the car park in Ashford walk back to the road and turn right up Vicarage Lane for about ¼ mile. At the top turn left along Highfields.

2. Follow the track, which becomes Pennyunk Lane, for ¾ mile.

3. Go through the squeeze stile and turn left up the field. At the top go through a gate and turn right.

4. Continue in the same direction passing a dew pond and going through small gates. This section is part track and part field.

5. After the last gate you come to two seats. Here you can picnic, rest and admire the view before returning to Ashford, or continuing down to Monsal Head.

For car directions to Monsal Head from Ashford see the "Monsal Head and the Longstones" venue page 39.

BAKEWELL

Directions

The main Bakewell car park is at the Agricultural Business Centre. As you approach Bakewell from Matlock turn right off the A6. Follow The Agricultural Way and the town car park route. Opposite the first building on the right there is disabled parking. Grid Ref SK221687

Description

Bakewell is known as The Capital of the Peak and its five-arch bridge dates back to the 13th century.

Jane Austen is reputed to have stayed at the Rutland Arms while writing Pride and Prejudice and in the 19th century a cook at the Rutland Arms misread a recipe for jam tarts, putting the jam mixture in first and accidentally creating the town's most famous export, the Bakewell pudding [or tart!].

The market [held every Monday] is a lively affair and Bakewell Show held every year in August attracts many visitors.

Bakewell has a lot to offer in the way of refreshment outlets, retail shops, the Visitor and Information Centre and a riverside walk. Most of the cafés and inns, however, do have small steps at their entrance. The "NICE" café in Kings Street is aiming to have disabled facilities. The "Felicini" at Rutland Mill off Coombs Road has all the facilities. To visit this Italian Restaurant you could park at the Bakewell Bridge Car Park [no concessions]. The "Felicini" is at the back of the car park.

While in Bakewell you might like to visit "Bakewell Old House Museum". It is situated behind the church and there is limited parking on the road. Blue badge holders may park on the Museum forecourt. It is advisable to telephone for advice on access ☎ 01629 813642.

Riverside Linear

A flat tarmac path with seats along the way from where you can watch the numerous birds on the river.

Route Instructions

From the town car park follow the signs for the town centre.

Pass the toilets [disabled not in use when this book was researched!]. After the second bridge you can turn left or right, to walk on a flat riverside path.

River Wye and Monsal Trail North
Circular 3 ½ miles

An undulating walk along tracks, a trail, and across fields with gates and stiles.

Route Instructions

1. Walk into the town from the main town car park off the Agricultural Way. Join the main A619 and turn right. Walk to and across the bridge over the River Wye.

2. Almost immediately, by the ornate lamp standard, go through the metal gate on the left.

3. Follow the riverside path and where the river meanders away left keep straight on. Go through the gate and continue ahead aiming for the houses. Go through a small gate onto the road and turn left.

4. Follow the minor road to the packhorse bridge.

5. Turn right opposite the bridge.

6. Walk up a wide partly surfaced track to pass the entrance to Holme Hall. The track bends round to the left and passes the old workings where stone was prepared for pottery making.

7. Continue up the stony shaded bridleway. Pass through a farmgate to leave the

wooded area. Keep straight on up the hill ignoring a track off left and crossing a stile by a farmgate.

8. Continue along and down a walled track for about ¾ mile crossing a stile and gates to reach the Monsal Trail.

9. Turn right to follow the Trail for about 1 ¼ miles. You will pass the entrance into Hassop Café and Book Shop. There are a number of seats along the trail.

10. At Bakewell Station turn right to leave the trail

11. Walk through the station car park then turn left.

12. Follow Station Road back to Bakewell.

River Wye and Monsal Trail South Circular 2 miles

A relatively easy route along the Wye Valley meadows and Monsal Trail. There is one short uphill field climb and stiles and gates. It would be advisable to take this route after a period of dry weather.

Route Instructions

1. From the main town car park walk back towards the Agricultural Way.

2. Follow a path by the hedge and fence close on the left, walking parallel to the Agricultural Way until it bends right, where you continue straight on by the hedge.

3. Cross a stile, a field and then through a small gate.

4. After the gate turn sharp left over a footbridge and then turn right. Veer away slightly from the hedge on your right. Cross two footbridges to the left of a small gate.

5. Follow the footpath sign keeping the hedge and stream close on the right and go through a small gate.

6. Turn left up the field and go through a gate. At the junction with a track turn left.

7. Follow the track for about ¼ mile to a T-junction with a minor road.

8. Turn left then almost immediately turn right signed Monsal Trail. Walk up a wide partly stepped path to the trail and turn left.

9. In nearly ¾ mile and just after walking under a bridge turn right up steps, and then turn right again across the bridge via a gate and stile.

10. Follow a hedge and fence close on the left down the field to join a track.

11. Go through a small gate by the farmgate. Continue down a surfaced drive to reach Coombs Road via a gate.

12. Turn right along the pavement and at the Public Footpath sign turn left to follow a surfaced path back to the car park.

Monsal Trail Hassop Station Linear 1¼ miles

Route to Bakewell Station

In the centre of Bakewell follow the A619 to drive along the one-way section then over the bridge. Turn right immediately after the bridge to drive up Station Road, the B6048. Park in the old station car park. There is disabled parking but no toilet facilities.

An easy, mainly flat walk along the hard shale surface of the trail.

Route Instructions

Pass the pay machine to join the trail and either turn right for a "there and back" stroll along the trail; or for Hassop Station Book Shop and Café turn left.

On the Hassop route the first part of the trail has a slight rise, after which it is flat. As you near the Hassop Café there are a number of seats and a picnic table.

Just before the bridge and café turn right into and across the car park to the front of the building. There are disabled and baby changing toilets at the café.

To drive to Hassop Café from Bakewell follow the A619 for about ¾ mile from the bridge then turn left onto the B6001 Hathersage road. In another ¾ mile at the roundabout turn right to take the fourth exit into the car park. Grid Ref SK 218706 There is disabled parking but no concessions. If you visit the book store and/or the café there is free parking in front of the building.

From this car park you can take another there and back stroll. Turn right from the small gate at the back of the café to walk along the flat trail towards Great Longstone or left back towards Bakewell.

BIRCHOVER AND STANTON MOOR

Directions

From Bakewell take the A6 Matlock route. In 2½ miles turn right onto the B5056 to Youlgrave. In about ¾ mile follow the B road as it bends round left over the bridge. In another 1½ miles turn up left signed "Birchover". To reach the car park drive up through the village. At the quarries take the left fork. The car park is a few metres along this road. Grid Ref SK 242628

Description

Birchover is a pleasant village on the edge of Stanton Moor where there are historical, archaeological and geological features to investigate. A number of information boards set at points of interest explain the history of the area. There are many side paths as this is an area of open access. Do take care round the old overgrown quarry sites. There are two inns in the village "The Red Lion" and "The Druid Inn" named after the Rowter Rocks behind the inn which are thought to have Druid connections. There is relatively easy access to The Druid but you would be advised to telephone them first ☎ 01629 650302. Similarly with The Red Lion where the access is quite good ☎ 01629 650363.

Stanton Moor Circular 2 miles

There are a number of easy mainly flat sandy paths, with stiles, across this historic site. This walk is not suitable for pushchairs but would be of interest to children.

Route Instructions

1. Leave the car park via the main entrance and turn left up the road.
2. In about 400 metres turn right across the stile by the footpath and Open Access signs. Keep straight on to cross another stile.
3. Follow the Stanton Moor path uphill for 200 metres to The Cork Stone. Turn left and in a few metres, at a fork of paths, bear left through the heather. You will pass the overgrown old quarry areas before entering the open birch woodland.
4. Where you enter a more open area you will see a fence ahead; just before this fence turn right to stay on the main path. This path soon narrows as it crosses the heather. At a fence corner stay on the main path as it bends round to the right. Soon you will pass The King Stone before walking by The Nine Ladies Circle.
5. At an information board cross a wide path to keep straight on. At a fork of paths bear left walking towards the Tower.
6. On reaching the Tower cross the stile on the left and pass the Tower also on your left. Go down the steps to the "Stanton Moor National Trust" sign.
7. Turn right to follow the path along the top of the escarpment with an old fence close on your right. After about ¾ mile, and at the next National Trust sign, turn right over a fence stile.
8. Turn left, ignoring a right-hand path, to walk through the heather. At the next crossings of paths turn left down the wider stony path to cross a stile onto the road.
9. Turn right to follow the road for about ¾ mile, ignoring the road down into Birchover, to return to the car park.

10. If you wish to walk into the village for refreshments before going back to the car then you can return to the car park along a path opposite The Druid this will add about 1 mile to the walk.

LATHKILL DALE

Directions
There are three parking areas for these Lathkill Dale walks.

Description
Lathkill Dale is very pretty in the summer and the paths are quite good in places for smaller wheelchairs and pushchairs, starting at Conksbury Bridge. The upper section of the dale is very rocky and narrow before coming out into a wider grassy dale to reach the road into Monyash.

Lathkill Dale Linear

Directions to Conksbury Bridge
From the centre of Bakewell by The Rutland Arms turn left onto the B5055 Monyash road. In about 1 mile turn left. Follow this secondary road for 1½ miles to descend in two steep bends towards the river. By the first bend there is a parking layby and a few metres further on, just before Conksbury Bridge, there is a parking place for one blue badge holder on the right behind the footpath post.

A pleasant flat shale path as far as you wish. It is about ¾ mile to the minor road leading up into Over Haddon. This ½ mile minor road is unsuitable for any one finding hill climbing difficult as it is very steep.

Over Haddon Circular 3 ½ miles

Directions to Over Haddon
From Bakewell follow the route as above but after about 1mile keep straight on for nearly ¼ mile then turn left to Over Haddon. In the village take a right turn then a left turn following the parking signs to the car park. There is disabled parking and toilets with a radar key. To reach the Lathkill Hotel turn left out of the car park then right at the T-junction and at the next T-junction turn left to follow a minor road. Just before a bend behind the hotel there is parking for hotel customers,

there is unofficial parking in front of the hotel. The hotel is in a superb position with extensive views over Lathkill Dale, a lovely place for a refreshment stop. It is built on a slope and there are six steps up into the hotel. They are very willing to offer help should it be needed.

A relatively easy walk across fields before walking above the beautiful Lathkill Dale where there are wonderful views to enjoy while you picnic. The only rather steep climb is up the last two fields back to the hotel. There are 16 stiles, most of them are quite easy.

Route Instructions

1. Leave the car park in Over Haddon via the main entrance to cross the road and walk up Dale Road to join Main Street. Keep straight on passing "Geoff's Diner". Cross the end of Bakewell Road to keep straight on. Walk behind the Lathkill Hotel and round the bend to cross a stile on the left in a wall corner.
2. Keep straight on up the field to cross a wall and fence stile to the left of a gate.
3. Bear right down the field aiming for two gateways and a wall corner. Cross the stile near the left-hand gateway. Follow the wall close on the left to cross the stile in the field corner and bear slightly left across the next field.
4. Cross the road via two gated stiles then bear left across the field corner to go over a high wall stile. Cross a track and walk on up the field to follow a wall on your left down the large field. Cross the high wall stile near the field corner. You will see a wood over to the right.
5. Bear right down the middle of the next field. Aim for a gate and a fence corner then follow the fence on the right to go through a small gate by the wall ahead.
6. Walk up the next two fields following the wall on the left and crossing the stile a few metres to the right of the first field corner.
7. As you approach the farm walk under the trees to go through a small gate or over the wall stile.
8. Bear right across the field following the "Over Haddon" route. From here you will be aiming for the white building of the Lathkill Hotel. Cross three fields, four stiles and a minor road.
9. Walk above the River Lathkill before going through the small gate in the fence on your right. Bear left to start your ascent to the village. Cross two fields and a gated stile under the hawthorn tree before crossing another gated stile onto the road.
10. Walk in front of the hotel then bear right up to the junction where you keep straight on to join Main Street. Keep straight on again to return to the car park.

Monyash and Upper Lathkill Dale Circular 2 miles

Directions to Monyash

From Bakewell take the B5055 to Monyash. In 5 miles turn right at the crossroads in the centre of the village. The small parking area is on the left.

A relatively easy slightly undulating walk. The route takes you along tracks and fields with stiles and gates before descending into the upper grassy section of the dale. This is a lovely walk with wonderful views.

The Bulls Head offer snacks and full meals in the bar or the refurbished dining room, all on the flat and there are disabled toilets. Opening times for meals Mon-Fri 12-2pm and weekends food all day. "The Old Smithy Tearooms and Bistro" next door offer drinks and tasty snacks, they also have disabled toilets and all areas are on the flat. Opening times 10am-5pm. Opposite the car park is a children's play area.

Route Instructions

1. Turn right from the car park and at the crossroads keep straight on along Rakes Road. Pass the meres where there is a seat for feeding the ducks!

2. After ¼ mile, where the road bends right keep straight on along a track. In about 50 metres bear left at a waymarked post.

3. Walk along a winding walled track for about ½ mile. At the end of the track go through a small gate.

4. Follow a path with a wall on the right to cross a gated stile on the right by the sign "Limestone Way".

5. Turn left down and up a field to cross Fern Dale. Go through a gated stile.

6. Keep straight on up the next two fields keeping a wall on the left and going through a gate. In the second field cross a wall stile on the left.

7. Continue following the Limestone Way with a wall now on the right.

8. At a farmgate turn left [not through it!]. Follow a farm track signed Lathkill Dale.

9. Go through a wide wall gap and keep straight on to go through another wall gap.

10. Follow a wall on the right. Go through a small gated stile and continue ahead aiming for the rocks down in Lathkill Dale. The wide grass path gradually bends left as it descends gently to the dale.

11. Cross a wall stile and turn left. This is a good picnic spot. Walk up the gradually ascending dale to reach the road going through three gates.

12. At the B5055, where there is parking and disabled toilets, turn left up the road back into the village. As you enter the village there is a plaque giving interesting details about Monyash and its surroundings.

Other interests

"Monyash The Making of a Derbyshire Village" is a fascinating, easy to read book which you can purchase from Shirley Johnston ☎ 01629 812575.

Arbor Low is an English Heritage site. To reach the site drive from the car park back to the crossroads and keep straight on along The Rakes. Follow this road for about 1 ¾ miles and just before reaching the A515 turn left to follow the brown signs, in about ¾ mile turn right up a farm track. Just before the farm there is a parking area. From here you walk through the farm through a gate and turn left up the field. There is a plaque explaining the site by the next gate.

After visiting this site you can either return to Bakewell or continue to the A515 and turn left to Ashbourne.

MONSAL HEAD AND THE LONGSTONES

Directions

From Bakewell take the A6 Buxton road. In 1 ½ miles turn right on the A6020 then left into Ashford-in-the-Water on the B6465 which almost immediately turns right signed Monsal Head. Follow this road for about 1 ¼ miles. Turn left into the Monsal Head Car Park, or continue for a few more metres to turn left into the short stay car park. There is disabled parking and toilets with your radar key.

Description

Monsal Head offers a viewing area with seats and ice cream! Hobb's Café and Gift Shop and the Monsal Head Hotel with its Stable Bar offering refreshments. There are no disabled facilities at the hotel or Stable Bar but the hotel are aiming to install them when the refurbishments have been completed ☎ 01629 640250. Hobb's café and craft shop has a ramp access but no disabled toilets, although they can be reached from the café.

The Packhorse Inn in Little Longstone has no disabled facilities and steep steps into the inn.

The Crispin Inn in Great Longstone offer flat parking facilities and a ramp into the cosy inn. The proprietors are used to helping disabled people if necessary. At The White Swan a ramp can be put in place at the side entrance.

The walks from here are for the more active and young families not dependent on pushchairs.

Monsal Head Circular 3 ½ miles

A challenging walk where you will be rewarded with wonderful views after a steep climb up from the viaduct. A delightful but steep woodland path takes you down into Monsal Dale with towering woodlands on both sides. This easy riverside walk will refresh you for the climb back up to Monsal Head. There are four squeeze and wall stiles.

Route Instructions

1. From the main Monsal Head Car Park walk up the passage-way between the hotel and the Stable Bar. Turn left and opposite the cafe go through the wider wall gap. Turn right down the stone steps. In a few yards turn left to continue down the path signed "Viaduct & Monsal Trail".

2. Turn right across the viaduct and just past the end turn left through the first small gate to follow the Brushfield route.

3. Walk up the steep rocky path. At a bridleway sign on the right continue up the stony and rocky track. At the top pass through a gate. If you divert a few metres to the left you will have wonderful views. Return to the track for another ½ mile.

4. Pass through a stile by a gate then follow the wall close on the left to cross another stile by a gate. In a few metres, and passed a wide wall gap, cross a wall stile on the right. [not easily seen, if you reach the field corner you have passed it!].

5. Having crossed the stile keep straight on across the field to go through a gate/gateway by the waymarked post.

6. Walk down the Brushfield Hough farm drive passing farm buildings. Just before the last building on the left turn left through the gate/gateway. Walk across the yard to turn right through another gate then the gateway ahead.

7. Bear left to join a track by a footpath post and turn right. Where the track bends right veer left off the track to cross a wall stile.

8. Turn right [a good picnic spot], to follow a grassy path down through the scrub. Soon the path bears round to the left and becomes more definite.

9. Descend the steep wooded hillside taking care especially if the path is wet. As you near the bottom of the hill the path becomes stepped. At a fork of paths take the right fork down to the Monsal Dale path.

10. Turn left to walk along Monsal Dale. In about 15 to 20 minutes the dale opens out. Fork right down to the footbridge below the weir.

11. Cross the footbridge and turn left.

12. Walk through the woods passing the weir and going through a gate. Continue uphill for about ½ mile back to Monsal Head.

The Weir Circular 1 ½ miles

Another challenging but rewarding walk. First there is a gradual descent to the dale then an easy dale walk before you ascend via the viaduct back to Monsal Head. There is one squeeze stile. Not suitable for pushchairs.

Route Instructions.

1. From the main Monsal Head Car Park walk to the viewing area and go through the widest gap.
2. Turn left signed "Ashford and Monsal Dale". Walk down the six steps then take the righthand fork of paths downhill.
3. Gradually descend across the valleyside going through two gates. On reaching the weir continue along the path to cross the footbridge.
4. Turn right to walk along the dale with the River Wye on the right. Go through a gate. Soon you will see the viaduct ahead.
5. Keep straight on to go through a stile by a gate and walk under the viaduct.
6. Follow the riverside path as it bends round to the left.
7. Just before the footbridge turn left at a waymarked post on the left and, turning back on yourself, follow a short steep path.
8. At the top of the path turn left to cross the viaduct.
9. At the tunnel turn left to walk up the path and at the junction with another path coming up from the dale turn right back up to Monsal Head.

Little Longstone Circular 3 miles

This route takes you through Little Longstone and to the north of Monsal Head via a gentle climb up a wide stony track. There are wall and squeeze stiles, eight in all.

The return paths are down fields where the views are extensive over Monsal Dale and south to Ashford. A short walk back along the road brings you to Monsal Head.

The packhorse Inn is a convenient refreshment stop but there are no disabled facilities.

Route Instructions

1. From the main Monsal Head Car Park walk back to the B6465 and turn left then almost immediately turn right. Walk down the road to and through Little Longstone. In about ¾ mile from Monsal Head turn left by the public footpath post just after "Orchard Cottage" and just before "Longstone Byre", the last house in the village.

2. Go up the walled track to cross a stile by a farmgate.

3. Turn right to follow the wall on the right crossing two fields and stiles.

4. Turn left up the track by Dale Farm for about 1 mile. As you near the top the views over to Monsal Head and beyond are splendid, there is also a seat where you can have a rest.

5. About 150 yards from the road ahead turn left to cross a stile and a small gate to follow the Little Longstone route.

6. Bear left across the middle of the field, aiming to the left of a single tree, to cross a stile near the wall corner. Keep straight on following the wall on the left and going through a small kissing gate.

7. After crossing the line of a broken wall ahead you will veer away from the wall on the left to have a broken wall on the right. The route descends the field to cross a stile.

8. Bear left around the hillside passing an old barn over to the right, then on down the field aiming for a stile in the wall ahead and passing a dew pond on the right.

9. Cross the stile in the field corner and continue in the same direction aiming for Little Longstone. Go through a small kissing gate ahead.

10. Follow a wall close on the right until you reach a stile in the wall. Cross this stile and turn left, the wall is now on the left. In a few yards bear off right down to and through a small gated stile. [This is a rather an undetermined area and may have friendly horses in it!]

11. Walk down past the barns then along a narrow shale path by the inn garden. When you reach the road turn right to retrace your outward route back to Monsal Head.

Little and Great Longstone Circular 2 ½ miles

This is an easy route across fields to the pretty village of Great Longstone. You might like to take a detour into the village where you will find The White Lion and The Crispin Inns. Turn left to join the Monsal Trail. After a short walk along the trail you will cross fields to Little Longstone. Return via your outward route back to Monsal Head. If you wish to use the newly opened tunnel to the viaduct you will have a steep climb back to Monsal Head.

Route Instructions

1. From the main Monsal Head Car Park walk to the entrance and turn left then almost immediately turn right down the B6465.

2. In Little Longstone continue down the road passing the inn. Opposite "Little Longstone Barns" turn right.

3. Cross the left-hand wall stile or go through the small gate by the footpath post. Ignore the Monsal Trail sign to bear up the hill following the Great Longstone route. As you near the top of the hill you will see a small fence enclosure on the right. Continue aiming for a fence stile ahead.

4. Cross the stile to walk along a short path to and through a small waymarked gate.

5. Walk almost diagonally across the next field aiming for a stile in the wall ahead and passing a single tree over to the right.

6. Cross the stile then the track to go through a small gate. Keep straight on for a few yards, with a wall on the left, to go through another gate.

7. Continue in the same direction across the middle of the next field. Go through a small gate in the wall ahead. Follow the field boundary on the left to cross a stile.

8. On reaching the village road in Great Longstone turn right.

9. [If you wish to visit the village turn left then follow the road, and at the road junction turn right into Great Longstone. To rejoin the circular route follow a path to the left of the White Lion which takes you through the large car park. Turn right by the school playground to walk between the houses. At the road junction turn left].

10. Follow the road to just past the derestriction sign and cross the gated stile on the right.

11. Bear left across the field walking between a line of trees, passing an old squeeze stile, and then go through a gate back onto the road.

12. Turn right and just before the bridge turn right down a flight of steps to the Monsal Trail at Thornbridge. Turn right to follow the trail and at the crossing of paths to Ashford and Little Longstone turn right over a wall stile. [The tunnel opened in spring 2011]

13. Turn left to follow a wall on the left. Go through a gate and keep straight on going through two gates,

14. At the road in Little Longstone turn left to retrace your outward route.

Great Longstone Circular 3 ½ miles

Directions to Great Longstone by car

Leave the Monsal Head Car Park to turn left then immediately right. Drive to and through Little Longstone. In Great Longstone park where convenient.

If you are visiting The White Lion you can use their large parking area at the back of the inn.

A relatively easy walk across fields and stiles with a mile stretch along the trail.

In May the village holds its annual flower festival during which time you can enjoy a snack in the village hall along Church Lane. Tel: The White Lion for details ☎ 01629 640252

Route Instructions

1. Opposite The White Lion walk along Church Lane to go through the churchyard gate on the right. At the road turn right for a few metres then turn left onto a track and almost immediately turn right through a squeeze stile.

2. Cross the corner of the field to go through another stile.

3. Turn right along a track. Where it bends left keep straight on through another squeeze stile.

4. Continue in the same direction across undulating fields. You will cross 8 squeeze stiles, 2 wall stiles, 3 tracks and a barn.

5. When you reach the road at the outskirts of Rowland turn right to walk down to the road junction. Turn left then immediately right.

6. Follow a track with the high Hassop estate wall on the left. Continue following this wall crossing a broken wall a squeeze stile and a fence stile. At a telegraph pole bear off right down the field aiming to the right of Toll Bar House.

7. Cross the wall stile and turn left along the road. Opposite Toll Bar House turn right through the farmgate.

8. Walk across the field to go through a small gate and turn right along the Monsal Trail.

9. In about 1 mile, at Thornbridge Station, leave the trail to climb a flight of steps to the road where you turn left.

10. In about 150 metres turn left through a gate. Bear slightly right across the field passing through a line of trees then aim for the road via a gated stile.

11. Turn left to follow the road for about 250 metres. Turn right along a tarmac path passing the school playground. At a T-junction of paths turn left to the White Lion car park and on down to the road.

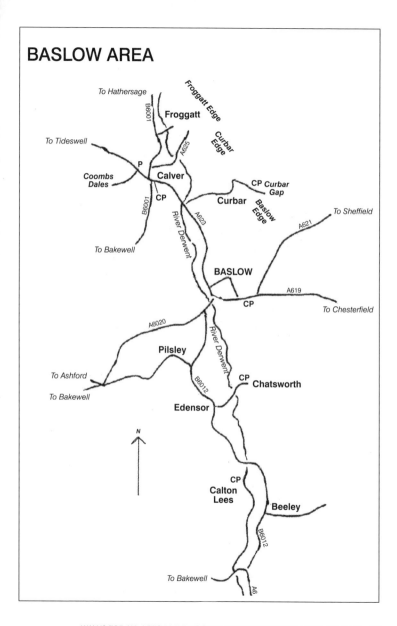

BASLOW AREA

To Hathersage

Froggatt Edge

B6001

Froggatt

Curbar Edge

To Tideswell

A625

Coombs Dales

P

Calver

CP

Curbar Gap

CP

Curbar

Baslow Edge

A621

To Sheffield

B6001

River Derwent

A623

To Bakewell

BASLOW

A619

CP

To Chesterfield

A6020

River Derwent

Pilsley

To Ashford

To Bakewell

B6012

CP

Chatsworth

Edensor

N

CP

Calton Lees

Beeley

B6012

To Bakewell

A6

BASLOW AREA

BASLOW & CURBAR

Directions

As you approach Baslow from Chatsworth turn right at the junction with the A623 to reach the Nether End [east] side of Baslow. At the traffic lights leave the A road to follow the right-hand fork where you turn right into the car park. Grid Ref SK 258721. Disabled parking and toilets. £4 for 4 hours, free for blue badge holders.

Description

The 17th century bridge at Bridge End, and guardhouse previously occupied by the toll-collector, spans the River Derwent.

At nearby Calver the former mill, which dates back to the 18th century, has now been converted into apartments. In the 1970s the mill was used as the setting for Colditz Castle in the television series. There is a local custom that the men of Baslow must climb the Eagle Rock on Baslow Edge before they are worthy of marriage.

Nether End Baslow has a choice of restaurants. The Devonshire Arms has a large car park, disabled access and toilets. The café has no disabled facilities.

Curbar Circular 3 miles

You will walk up minor roads [one short stretch is about 1in8], along tracks and across fields with 2 squeeze stiles and one short stretch along the pavement by the A623. This walk will reward you with wonderful views.

Route Instructions

1. From the car park cross the green and the A619 to walk up Eaton Hill.
2. At the top of the hill turn right up Bar Lane and in about 100 metres turn left up Gorse Bank Lane.
3. Follow the surfaced lane to the farm. Walk through the farmyard and keep straight on to go through a small gate.
4. Continue in the same direction along a walled track, part of which is an old stone path.
5. At the end of the track go through a squeeze stile and bear slightly left to go through a gateway. Follow a wall then a fence close on the left going through two gateways.

6. Bear left for a few metres to go through another gate. Walk diagonally across and down the next field to go through a gated stile.

7. Keep the wall on the left and where it bends left keep straight on to go through a small gate. Turn right keeping a wall close on the right. Go through another gated stile and walk up the walled path. Where the path splits take the right-hand path up and round a bend.

8. Pass through another gate and bear right to join a surfaced drive and continue up the drive. You will notice a conical roofed building over to the right. This is an old jail house where prisoners were kept overnight on their way to the courts in Derby.

9. On reaching the road in Curbar Village turn left downhill. At the crossroads turn left up Cliff Lane.

10. Follow the tarmac lane downhill, passing Cliff College, to the A623.

11. Turn left along the pavement of the A623 for nearly ¼ mile. Bear left up Over Lane. This minor road is quite steep in places [one short stretch is about 1in 8].

12. In about ¾ mile you will reach Over End Baslow. Continue on down to the T-junction where you turn left up School Lane passing the Spar shop.

13. At the road junction turn right to retrace your outward route down Eaton Hill back to the car park.

Curbar Edge   Linear and 3 miles

Directions to Curbar Gap Car Park

From Baslow follow the A623 to Curbar [1 ¼ miles] and turn right just before the Bridge Inn [refreshment and disabled access and parking]. Turn right up Curbar Lane signed "Curbar Village".

Follow this steep uphill road for about 1 mile, passing laybys on the left. At the top of the hill turn left into the pay and display car park Grid Ref SK 262747. From the first parking area there is wheelchair access to Baslow Edge and from the second parking area there is wheelchair access to the picnic area.

This is easily one of our favourite view points and walks. The open ruggedness and long views are conducive to bringing peace and happiness. Here the forces of nature in this world of ours are very positive and uplifting.

Directions to The Grouse Inn from Curbar Gap Car Park

Return to the A623 and turn right to Calver village. At the crossroads turn right on to the A625 follow this road which after a few metres branches off right signed Froggatt. In just over 2 miles turn left into The Grouse Inn car park. There is ample parking and the access is easy but there are no disabled toilets. The views from the outdoor eating area are wonderful.

Route Instructions for picnic area and the Grouse Inn

1. From the second car parking area at Curbar Gap follow the path at the back keeping a wall on the right. In about 200 metres you come to a wide grass area with picnic tables and seats and wonderful views.

2. If you wish for a stroll along the edge cross a small embankment to walk up a very short stone slabbed path to go through a gate.

3. Follow the edge path as far as you wish. There are many large flat rocks where you can picnic. This is a favourite area for rock climbers.

4. If you wish to visit the Grouse Inn follow the edge path across Curbar and Froggatt Edges to the A625 then continue up the road to the inn. This will give you nearly a 3 mile walk.

Route Instructions for Baslow Edge

1. From the first parking area at Curbar Gap follow the wheelchair route to cross the road and up a short path to go through a gate.

2. Follow a wide compacted path passing a seat to take the right-hand path.

3. In a few metres you will reach the viewing point where you can sit on the low wall.

4. Return to the main path and then you can either return to the car park or continue along the rather stonier track to the Eagle Stone [¾ mile] or Wellington Monument [1 mile] where there are seats with more wonderful views over towards Chatsworth. This longer route is not suitable for wheelchairs and there is no pick up point.

Baslow Edge Circular 2 miles

An Edge walk with wonderful views and only one stile. There is quite a steep climb at the end of the route.

Follow the car route to Curbar Gap Car Park as described on page 47.

Route Instructions

1. From the car park at Curbar Gap follow the sign for wheelchairs to Baslow Edge.

2. Cross the road to go up a slight rise and along a path to go through a gate.

3. Pass a seat to follow a wide stony track for 1 mile, passing the Eagle Stone.

4. At a junction of tracks turn right [unless you want to visit Wellington Monument].

5. Walk down a stony track passing a viewing seat up on the right. In about 300

metres turn right below rock outcrops.

6. Follow the rough bridleway which soon bends round to the right. The route becomes smoother as it gradually descends on a wide grass track below Baslow and Blackstone Edges.

7. In about 400 metres at footpath No. 311 keep to the upper track signed Curbar Edge.

8. The next section of the bridleway is stony and more irregular and it may be quite muddy, especially at a gateway further along.

9. After the gateway at a fork of tracks/paths take the right-hand higher route across the moorland.

10. Aim for and through the gate ahead walking through the bracken.

11. Keep straight on with a wall up on the right. In about 100 metres turn right to cross the squeeze stile.

12. Bear left to a wall corner. Follow a wall on the left which leads you up steps. Bearing left follow the path to the road which you reach via a gate.

13. Turn right to follow a narrow path parallel to the road until you see a footpath post on the left-hand side of the road. Cross the road to follow a wide sandy and stony track up and round a bend.

14. Turn right to pass a picnic area and keeping a wall on the left, back to the car park.

Baslow to Curbar Linear 1 ¾ miles

Directions to parking area near Baslow church

From the Nether End Car Park return to the crossroads and keep straight on into Baslow village. There is a small parking area on the left by the church. Grid Ref 252724

There are a variety of shops to visit and two refreshment stops with some disabled facilities. The Rutland Arms and Charlies Café and Bistro both with flat parking areas although the café parking is small and should be used only for disabled parking where there is easy access at the rear of the café.

Route Instructions

1. From the parking area turn left, leaving the main road, to cross the old toll bridge and turn right. Follow the minor road for nearly ¾ mile. Where the road bends left go through a gate on the right.

2. Follow the riverside path across the water meadows. Go through a gate and two squeeze stiles to continue ahead crossing a footbridge via a gate.

3. Walk along a surfaced path passing houses on the left. This path takes you down under the roads to the minor slip road leading to The Derbyshire Craft Centre and Café.

4. Return via the same route or you can be picked up outside the café. To drive to this point follow the A623 from Baslow and after passing the Bridge Inn turn right to the Craft Centre.

CALVER

Directions

From Baslow continue north on the A623 for 2 miles to the centre of Calver passing through Curbar.

There is no official parking, but you can park near the Derwent Arms and to reach it from the main Calver crossroads turn left and left again to take the residential road known as Sough Lane. The parking area is on your right. Grid Ref SK 240747 The Derwent Arms, opposite the parking area, has flat parking and wheelchair access at the back of the inn but no disabled toilets. The short minor road in Calver between the A623 and the A625 is often used by motorists for parking.

Description

Calver is a small village at the crossroads of the A623 between Baslow and Eyam and the Bakewell Hathersage Froggatt roads. The Eyre Arms, Hassop has disabled parking, access and toilets also a family room. This inn caters for the senior citizen. The "Outside" shop has a café attached with disabled facilities. On the Stoney Middleton road [A623] is a shoes and clothing discount store with a ramp access.

Froggatt Circular 3 miles

An easy walk mainly along the flat riverside paths, some stretches of which could be very muddy although improvements are being made. Part of the route is through a wildlife area.

The surfaced track from Calver Mill Gallery to Instruction 6 is suitable for wheelchairs. The route from instructions 9 to 14 is gradually being improved [funding permitting].

Route Instructions

1. From the parking area by the Derwent Arms turn left out of the entrance and immediately right to continue along Sough Lane.

2. At the road junction turn left along Main Street. Follow this village road to the main A623.

3. Turn right, there are railings on the left. In about 150 metres, and just opposite The Derbyshire Craft Centre, turn right along Riverside Drive.

4. In about 100 metres turn left to follow a path between the houses then turn left again to walk under the road and by the river. Walk up to the road.

5. Cross the minor road to the Calver Mill Gallery [closed on Mondays].

6. Walk along the driveway passing the gallery on your right. At the barns and caravan site you leave the tarmac drive.

7. Go through the small gate by the farmgate and keep straight on across the field, crossing a small stream. Aim towards the river.

8. Follow the compact shale and stone riverside path. Go through a gate and round a boom to walk up a stony track to the road at New Bridge.

9. Cross the A625 to go through a wall gap and down a step then on down a very short stony path to a wider path.

10. Cross a footbridge on your right and turn right. Follow the river on the right through Calver Marsh Wildlife area [see notice boards], there are 2 gates and 1 stile.

11. When you reach Froggatt bridge bear left to go through a squeeze stile then turn right across the bridge. At the road junction turn right. In about 75 metres cross a wall stile via 4 steps.

12. Turn left to follow the river on your right. This path is due for restoration. At the end of this section of the riverside path – parts of which could be very muddy – there are steps to the road at New Bridge (a new path and gate are being constructed).

13. Cross the road to go through a stile. Continue along the partly shaled path which shortly climbs to cross a small footbridge. The path now becomes more undulating and uneven before flattening out by meadowland.

14. At the end of the riverside path go through a gate onto the road and turn right.

15. Walk down the minor road to The Bridge Inn where there is disabled parking and access but no disabled toilets although they are wide enough for wheelchairs.

16. Turn right to walk along the iron railed footbridge. Here you could make a slight diversion to visit the Derbyshire Craft Centre. They have a ramped access to the shop and the café, the latter is via the car park at the side of the building.

There are no disabled toilets.

17. Return to the end of the footbridge and cross the road to a tarmac path, take the left fork to walk under the bridge.

18. Follow your outward route back to the parking area in Calver Village.

Coombs Dale Linear

Directions to the start of the walk [walk or drive]

Leave the parking area by the Derwent Arms, return to the crossroads at the end of Sough Lane. Cross the B6001 Bakewell road and drive/walk along the A623 following the sign to Stony Middleton. In a few metres turn right along a minor road between the A623 and A625 by a field [often used for the display of tents]. Grid Ref SK 238747

A flat walk along a wide hard surfaced track.

The access for wheelchairs is difficult as there is no "ramp" off the pavement to cross the road to enter Coombs Dale.

Route Instructions

1. From the minor road parking turn right along the A623 towards Stoney Middleton, for nearly ¼ mile to turn left at the footpath and private signs. Walk along a surfaced track by the playing field.

2. Walk up to and round a gate, the track now becoming hard packed shale.

3. Follow the track as far as you wish and return.

Coombs Dale Circular 3 ½ miles

Park/start the walk as described in previous walk

A challenging route for the adventurous young child! At the start you have a climb of about 400ft up a rocky path then down a grassy path before following a track. There are gates and stiles.

Route Instructions

1. Walk back to the traffic lights in Calver and turn right up the B6001 Bakewell road for a few metres passing the entrance to the garden centre on your right. Almost immediately turn right over a stile by the gate to walk up a private drive. Cross another stile by a gate.

2. Continue ahead up the path and soon you will have a wall on the right as you climb the hill. Go through a gate.

3. Keep straight on gradually climbing the tree-lined rather rocky sunken path. Near the top of the path go through two small gates, crossing a field, to pass the gorse bushes. The distance from the road to this point is about ¾ mile and you will have done nearly all the climb.

4. Follow a fence then a wall on the left and just before a waymarked stile, by a gate, turn right.

5. Walk downhill towards the telegraph poles, which you pass on your right, then on down the valley to a waymarked post. Continue on a downward path with the wall on the left.

6. Eventually you cross a fence stile on the left and turn right on down the dale. Cross a large wooden stile and walk to the track ahead crossing a small stream.

7. Turn right along the wide partly surfaced track of Coombs Dale. In about ¾ mile you will go round a gate to walk to the A623 and turn right to walk back into Calver.

CHATSWORTH

Directions

From Baslow drive into Chatsworth via the A619 and the B6012. Follow the signs to Chatsworth House. Pass the kiosk [£2 parking] and park in the main car park. The toilets are at the entrance to the courtyard and in the restaurant where there are disabled toilets. The restaurant is open from Easter to Mid-December.

Description

Chatsworth has much to offer. A restaurant with disabled facilities, the gardens and the house as well as the farm. The driveways are tarmac and many of the paths are hard surfaced. Three walk routes have been suggested but you will find others that suit your needs.

Edensor Linear ½ mile

A walk across the park on an undulating hard surfaced path to Edensor. Joseph Paxton, designer of The Crystal Palace and head gardener of the 6th Duke of Devonshire is buried in the churchyard of St Peters Church. Kathleen Kennedy sister of President John F Kennedy, was married to the 10th Duke's eldest son, she is also buried in the churchyard.

The village shop, post office and tea room are worth a visit. Open: Wed–Sun. There are parking areas and toilets in the courtyard just past the tearoom but no disabled toilets.

Route Instructions

1. From the car park return to the kiosk and walk in front of the house entrance to follow a path back to the bridge via a gate.
2. Cross the bridge and the road to walk up the path on your right under the trees.
3. At the road junction cross to the blue gates.
4. Walk into Edensor bearing round to the left.
5. At the church wall turn left to the tea rooms and shop.

Calton Lees Linear 1 mile

A stroll to Chatsworth Garden Centre following the riverside undulating path to Calton Lees Car Park and down the drive to the Garden Centre. There are steps to some of the sales areas and the café. The toilets are on the flat at the entrance to the Garden Centre.

Route Instructions

1. From Chatsworth Car Park walk to and across the bridge.
2. Turn left off the estate drive to walk down to the riverside path.
3. Follow this undulating path for about ¾ mile before walking uphill away from the river.
4. Cross the road by the cattle grid to go through a small gate.
5. Follow the path to and through the car park. [Pick up area]
6. Bear off left down to the Garden Centre.

Baslow Linear 1 ¼ miles

Two routes are possible:–

1. A wheelchair stroll into Baslow along estate paths and drives. The gate will accept a small wheelchair

Route Instructions

1. From car park walk back to the kiosk and turn right.

2. Follow the tarmac driveway passing the no-entry sign. Stay on this flat drive until you see the large sign. At this point you can stay on the drive to the Golden Gate then retrace your steps or turn left across the grass, which is fairly flat and well used. In a few metres you will reach a gate.

3. Pass through a tall black circular gate and follow the path to Baslow Nether End crossing the bridge over Bar Brook.

There are a number of refreshment outlets, The Café on the Green [no disabled facilities] and The Devonshire Arms with disabled parking toilets and easy access.

2. A stroll along the riverside path

Route Instructions

1. From the car park walk to and past the house entrance.

2. Follow a path by the fence on the right to go through a gate and on up to the bridge.

3. Just before the bridge turn right then go through a gate. Pass Queen Mary's Bower on the right.

4. Follow the hard shale surfaced path, not very even in places, for about 1 mile. At a fork of paths bear up right.

5. Go through the black circular gate. Continue ahead on a wide driveway to Baslow Nether End where you turn left across the bridge.

Calton Lees Car Park Circular 4 miles

Directions to Calton Lees Car Park

From Chatsworth drive south through the park on the B6012. Immediately after crossing the cattle grid bear off right into the Calton Lees Car Park.

Although this is a longer walk it is relatively easy after the gradual climb up a track to Calton Houses. A welcome break at Edensor Tea Rooms or a picnic near the river, where there are seats, would be an enjoyable reward!

Route Instructions

1. From the southern end of the car park, by the entrance to the garden centre take a minor road.

2. In about 350 metres by the grass triangle in Calton Lees keep straight on to go through the middle of three gates with the sign "Keep dogs on leads".

3. Follow the wide track for about 1 mile as it gradually climbs up to Calton

Houses, where it takes a sharp right and left bend to a gate.

4. Go through the gate and past the dwellings. About 100 metres beyond the last cottage go through a gate and turn right.

5. Follow the wall close on your right for 200 metres then bear off left along the path up towards the wood passing Russian Cottage over to the right. Go through a farmgate to walk through New Piece Wood on a wide walled track. Cross the high walled stile by the gate.

6. Walk down the field to a waymarked post then on down, following the yellow waymarked arrow, to pass a fenced copse of trees over on the right. Continue downhill under the trees to pass another fenced copse also on the right. Where the fence bends round to the right keep straight on. You will see the spire of Edensor church ahead. Aim for the church. As you near the village keep the church over to the right. Aim for a small metal gate.

7. Climb the steps to go through the small metal gate and on down the steps into Edensor village. Turn right down the village road. [If you need refreshment and a toilet stop bear right to enter a short drive opposite the church, the toilets can be reached through a courtyard] Walk to the cattle grid and gates to go through a metal swing gate.

8. Cross the B6012 park road to follow the shale path which takes you to the bridge. [Do not cross the bridge unless you wish to visit the House and restaurant]

9. Turn right at the start of the bridge to take a path down towards the river.

10. Follow the undulating riverside path back to the Calton Lees Car Park.

Chatsworth

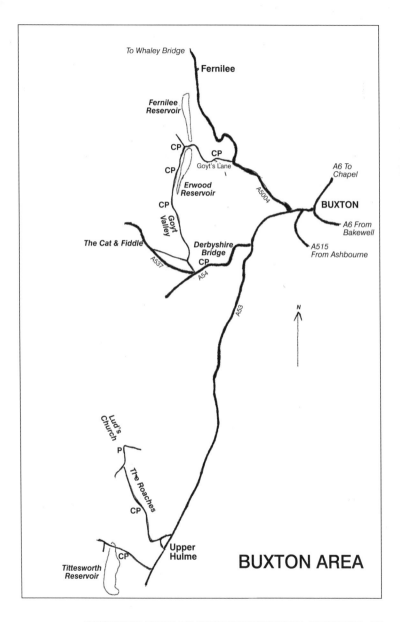

To Whaley Bridge

Fernilee

Fernilee Reservoir

CP

CP

CP

Goyt's Lane

Erwood Reservoir

A6 To Chapel

A5004

BUXTON

A6 From Bakewell

CP

Goyt Valley

Derbyshire Bridge

The Cat & Fiddle

A537

A54

CP

A515 From Ashbourne

A53

N

Lud's Church

P

The Roaches

CP

Upper Hulme

CP

Tittesworth Reservoir

BUXTON AREA

BUXTON AREA

BUXTON

Directions

To reach the main large car park from the centre of Buxton drive along the A53 Leek road for a short way to take a left turn then left again into the car park. The car park is behind Buxton Opera House and at the entrance to the Pavilion and Gardens. There is disabled parking and toilets. The approach to the Pavilion Gardens and the Pavilion with cafes, information and shops is all on the flat.

Description

Buxton stands 1000 feet above sea level and has been famous for its spa waters since the Romans built the baths in the first century AD. St Ann's Well is next to The Crescent commissioned by the 5th Duke of Devonshire in 1780. The Pavilion Gardens, on the banks of the River Wye are also worth a visit.

The Gardens Linear

The gardens are beautiful during the spring and summer and easily accessible with a wheelchair.

Buxton Country Park and Pools Cavern

Information for this visit can be obtained from the Information desk in the Pavilion.

To drive there turn left out of the car park then follow the signs to Poole's Cavern.

ERRWOOD AND FERNILEE RESERVOIRS

Directions

The Reservoirs

From the centre of Buxton take the A5004 Whaley Bridge road and in 2 ¼ miles take the first turn left after leaving Buxton signed Goyt Valley. Follow this minor road [Goyt's Lane] for 1 ½ miles down to the reservoirs. Just after crossing between them turn left then immediately right into the car park. There is disabled parking in a separate accessible tarmac area at the entrance to the car park. No toilets. The nearest are at Derbyshire Bridge [not disabled]. The road by the reservoirs is closed to cars between 11am and 5pm on Bank Holidays and from 1st May to 30th September.

Derbyshire Bridge and The Cat & Fiddle

To reach Derbyshire Bridge from Buxton take the A53 Leek road. In about 1 ½ miles and having driven through Burbage turn right onto the A54. Follow this road round the hillside [The Terret], for about 1 ¾ miles, then fork right onto the A537. In about 200 metres leave the main road at the white sign "Derbyshire Bridge [only]" to turn right. Drive down this narrow moorland road going round a sharp left-hand bend. At a T-junction turn right down to the car park and picnic area, or turn left to The Cat and Fiddle.

Description

The moorlands on either side of the Goyt River and Errwood Reservoir offer stunning views on a clear day. The climbs up onto the moors are gradual and on the whole the paths are clearly defined and signed. The paths along the reservoirs are hardsurfaced and tarmac in places, mostly suitable for wheelchairs. There are a number of inviting picnic spots in the Goyt Valley overlooking Errwood Reservoir.

Errwood Reservoir Linear ¾ mile, 1 ½ miles and 2 ½ miles to Derbyshire Bridge

After the main car park at the northern end of the reservoir, called "The Street", there are two more car parking areas off the minor road which follows the edge of the reservoir. Along some sections you can follow woodland paths which link up with the road. This is a beautiful area with many picnic spots.

Fernilee Reservoir Circular 3 miles

This is a relatively easy walk for most of the route along both sides of the reservoir. There is a steep road or very steep path at the end.

Route Instructions

1. From the car park walk up the blocked stone track to cross the exit point.
2. Keep straight on up a path with a wood on the left and walking parallel to the

road. Soon you cross a broken wall and then follow it on the left. In about ¼ mile from the car park the path leads down to the road.

3. Cross the road to two farmgates and go through the small gate.

4. Follow the sign to Fernilee and Hoo Moor. This route is now along a wide undulating hard packed stone track with no stiles or gates until the end of the track.

5. In 1 mile go through a gate and immediately turn right back on yourself, signed Fernilee.

6. Walk down the partly surfaced track to the dam and keep straight on along the dam road.

7. Turn right along the hard-packed track. It is rather stony in places. There are five seats along this flat track.

8. In 1 mile you have a choice of routes back to the car:-

1. Continue along and up the steep tarmac drive to the road where you turn right across the Errwood Dam road back to the car park. OR

2. Turn right through a gate to follow a path below the dam before climbing up a steep path. At a T-junction of paths turn left. Climb up another very steep path by a fence on the left. At the top of this path bear round to the left to go through a gate. Walk on up the field to the road and the car park.

Goyt's Lane & Wild Moor Linear

Directions to Goyt's Lane Car Park

Follow the route from Buxton to the reservoirs [as above] and about ¾ mile down Goyt's Lane turn right into the smaller car park ignoring the car park by the lake on the left. There are three disabled parking areas.

From the car park cross the road and go through a gate to the old railway track signed for wheelchair and footpath only.

The linear route is along a level path following the former Cromford and High Peak Railway into the wild moorland, an isolated and peaceful setting with wonderful views. There are benches along the way. It is 2 ¾ miles to the end of the track, but no pick up point.

LUD'S CHURCH AND THE ROACHES

Directions

From Buxton take the A53 through Burbage. Follow A53 road for about 8 ½ miles from the centre of Buxton. As you approach Upper Hulme you will see the towering rocks of Hen Cloud. Take the second right turn to Upper Hulme. Follow the twisting minor road through the village ignoring the right fork. Pass The Roaches Tea Rooms. There are two parking areas:-

The Roaches parking area is on the designated marked areas along the road below the ridge. There is 1 disabled parking place.

Lud's Church parking area continue past The Roaches parking areas for about 1 ½ miles following the minor road. After passing through a gate you should be able to find a parking space.

At Bank Holidays and weekends during school holidays it would be wise to arrive early at both these parking areas.

Description

The Roaches and Lud's Church routes are full of interest and wonderful views. The routes are suitable for people who can walk short distances and climb steep rocky steps.

If you wish for a more tranquil setting visit Tittesworth Reservoir Visitor Centre. See "Other Outings" page 96.

The Roaches Circular 4 miles

This walk has two distinct sections, 2 ½ miles across the edge and 1 ½ miles along a pleasant minor road.

For young children this would be an exciting route. The start of the route is through open woodland with some steep rocky climbs to reach the dramatic rocks of The Roaches. The views across the undulating edge are magnificent. The return route follows an easy minor road for about 1 ½ miles back to the parking area.

There are a number of picnic spots across The Roaches.

After your walk why not stop at The Roaches Tea Room for refreshments. They have a small parking area with toilets. The tea room is approached via a few steps but the café is all on one level. Open: Mar-Oct, 9am-5.30pm; Nov-Feb, 9am-4pm.

Route Instructions

1. From where you park return to the disabled area and a farmgate and small gate. Go through the small gate and turn right up the gravel path for about 200 metres then turn left.

2. Follow the path up to a wall which you follow for a few metres before going through a wall gap.

3. Keep straight on uphill with the wall of Rockhall on the right. At the old gate [Don Whillans] turn left continuing uphill and up the steep rock steps.

4. At the top turn left. Walk below the high rock outcrops then through open woodland for about 300 metres.

5. Turn right up the next steep rocky partly stepped path. At the top turn left.

6. Follow the undulating rocky path across The Roaches. In about 400 metres you will pass Doxy Pool. At the end of the edge follow a path down to the minor road at Bearstone Rock. From the pool to near Bearstone Rock, will take about 1 hour continuous walking.

7. Turn left to follow the quiet pleasant and gated minor road for nearly 1 ½ miles back to the parking area. The views from this road make it an enjoyable easy route at the end of the walk.

Doxy Pool on The Roaches

Lud's Church Circular 3 miles

An interesting route for the young family not needing a pushchair.

A walk beyond the rocky edge of The Roaches. The magnificent awe inspiring Lud's Church is reached by a rather steep flight of stone steps. The deep rocky cleft is about 100 metres long and only 2 metres wide. Over the years this cleft has offered shelter to many renegades. Robin Hood is thought to have used it. Followers of John Wycliff [a church reformer] used this remote cleft for worship in the 15th century, hence its current name. Soon after leaving Lud's Church a tall mound of rocks offers a suitable picnic area. The return route follows the gradually climbing moorland paths back to the start.

Route Instructions

1. This walk starts where the minor road bends round Bearstone Rock. With your back to Bearstone Rock and The Roaches and a track on the right walk up the steps ahead. Go through a stile and immediately cross a stile on the right.

2. Follow a wall on the right as you walk down the old stone and rocky path soon entering a wood. At the bottom of the path cross a stream to walk up to a footpath post.

3. Turn left signed "Lud's Church & Swythamley". Follow the woodland path for about ¾ mile as it contours the hillside. At the next footpath post turn left to Lud's Church. At a fork of paths take the right-hand path. This area may be muddy.

4. When you reach the deep rock cleft of Lud's Church follow the left-hand path which soon takes you down steps into the deep cleft. Follow the route through this awe inspiring natural rock cleft. This feature has been formed by a landslide, where a large section of rock has become detached from the hillside. As you walk through the 100 metres long narrow winding passage, the moss and fern covered rock sides tower over 15 metres [50ft] above you.

5. Leave the cleft by a short flight of steps and turn left. At the next signpost keep straight on following the clear moorland path, first in a westerly direction then turning south.

6. Ignore the first junction of paths signed The Roaches. Carry straight on and at the next junction of paths turn left signed The Roaches.

7. Follow the path below the Back Forest ridge keeping a wall on the right. In just over ¾ mile at a junction of paths continue ahead still following the Roach End route. Go through a small gate. At the next junction of paths bear round to the right to continue in the same direction. In another ½ mile go through a gate and back to the start of the walk.

CASTLETON AREA

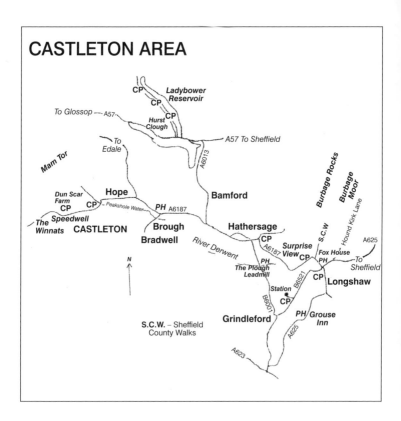

CP
Ladybower Reservoir
CP
CP
To Glossop — A57
Hurst Clough
A57 To Sheffield
To Edale
A6013
Mam Tor
Burbage Rocks
Burbage Moor
Dun Scar Farm
CP
Hope
CP — Peakshole Water
PH A6187
Bamford
Hound Kirk Lane
The Winnats
Speedwell
CASTLETON
Brough
Bradwell
Hathersage
River Derwent
A6187
S.C.W
A625
Surprise View CP
Fox House
PH
To Sheffield
N
PH
The Plough
Leadmill
CP
Longshaw
B6521
B6001
Station
CP
Grindleford
PH Grouse Inn
A625

S.C.W. – Sheffield County Walks

A623

CASTLETON AREA

CASTLETON

Directions

The main car park is at The Visitor Centre off the A6187 at the western end of the town. There is parking for 100 cars and 8 disabled spaces (which are free). There are toilets and disabled facilities with your radar key, an information centre, and a snacks kiosk.

Description

Castleton has much to offer the visitor. It is famous for Blue John mined there and the mines and caves are well worth a visit. There are wonderful views of the surrounding hills of Mam Tor, Hollins Cross and Lose Hill. The tea rooms and inns, retail shops especially those selling Blue John jewellery all add interest for the visitor. The Castle Inn has a flat entrance, disabled and baby changing toilets at the back and plenty of space. To reach the inn from the car park turn left up a short hill then take the first turn on the right.

The walks in the Hope Valley are relatively easy and you are able to enjoy the mountains and hills without the effort of climbing them! The walks are not suitable for push and wheelchairs.

Speedwell Circular 1 ½ miles

A pleasant walk along an undulating path below the hills before returning via fields or the A6187. Instruction 1 is suitable for wheelchairs as far as Goose Hill.

Route Instructions

1. From the car park return to and cross the main road. Follow the Riverside Walk, a surfaced path, to the minor road where you turn right. Cross the river bridge and walk up Goose Hill then on up to join a stony wooded track and go through a gate.

2. Follow an undulating path for ½ mile keeping a wall close on the right until you reach the road via a gate. Turn left for the caverns.

3. To continue the walk cross the road diagonally left to go over a stile by a gate.

4. Keep straight on, ignoring a right fork of grass paths, then almost immediately turn right at a crossing of paths. Go through a wall gap.

5. Bear round to the left aiming for the left-hand wall gap and stile. Cross the stile.

6. Turn right along the road for a few metres then left to follow a track which crosses a cattle grid.

7. Just by the next cattle grid turn right over two stiles.

8. Follow the stream on the left crossing two fields and stiles before bearing off right towards the houses. Go through a gate in the field corner.

9. Walk along a path between the buildings to the main road and turn left to the car park.

Dunscar Farm Circular 2 ¼ miles

An easy mainly flat route through the town and along tracks and fields with good views of the hills.

1. From the car park return to the main road and turn left to walk up through the town along the A6187. Go round a sharp left bend and where it bends right keep straight on.

2. Walk down the Hollowford road for about 300 metres then turn left at a farm track and almost immediately turn right.

3. Follow a stony track which soon becomes a shady sunken track.

4. Go through a farmgate and almost immediately turn left to follow a path with a wall on the right. Soon the path bends right.

5. Go through a gate by a farmgate and keep straight on. [You have good views of Winnats Pass and Mam Tor].

6. Continue in the same direction crossing two fields and gates to join the drive at Dunscar Farm.

7. Turn left down the drive and at a cattle grid turn left over two stiles.

8. Keep the wall and stream on the left as you cross two fields and stiles. In the third field bear right to go through a gate in the field corner.

9. Walk along a narrow path to the road and turn left back to the Visitor Centre.

Castleton to Hope Linear 2 miles

A very pleasant stroll in the Peakshole Water Valley crossing fields and stiles to the village of Hope, where there are a number of refreshment outlets and toilets. (see page 69)

Route Instructions

1. Turn left out of the car park to walk about ¾ mile through Castleton. You will go round two sharp bends, pass "Ye Olde Cheshire Cheese Inn" and turn right at the "Public Footpath Hope".

2. Follow the walled track which soon becomes a narrow path in the valley on Peakshole Water. Cross a stile then continue in the same direction with a fence on the left and after crossing a broken wall follow the fence on the right to cross a stile.

3. Keep straight on crossing fields, gates and stiles. Cross the railway line via two stiles.

4. Follow the well defined riverside path crossing stiles and gates until you reach the road; about 1 mile from Castleton. Turn left to walk up Pinfold Road into Hope.

5. The Blue Apple Café is on the right a few metres along the Edale Road and The Cheshire Cheese Inn is about ½ mile along the Edale Road.

6. **To reach the Hope Car Park from Castleton** drive through Castleton on the A6187. In about 1 ½ miles turn right into the car park where there is disabled parking and toilets using your disabled radar key.

HATHERSAGE

Directions

From Castleton drive back along the A6187 passing through Hope. About 2 ½ miles after Hope you pass the High Peak Garden Centre on the left. This is a pleasant visit with a café and all the extensive garden offerings. The site is on the flat and the café has easy access with disabled facilities. The small disabled parking area is on the left just past the main car park.

When you reach Hathersage turn right up the B6001. In about 300 metres turn left to the car park. Grid Ref. SK 232814 There are disabled parking areas.

Description

Before Victorian times this was a grim mill town, but by the mid 19th century Hathersage had become famous for its brass buttons. However, by the early 20th century it declined when Sheffield developed more advanced machinery. Charlotte Bronte stayed at the vicarage while writing Jane Eyre. In the novel Hathersage appears as Norton. It is also supposed to be the final resting place of Little John [of Robin Hood fame]. There is a head stone in St Michael's churchyard.

For the toilets walk to the bottom right-hand corner to follow a surfaced path to the main road where you turn left for the toilets + disabled toilets.

The George Hotel, further down the main road, has a good flat car park; the entrance, dining area and comfortable lounge are all on the flat also the toilets but there are no disabled toilets.

The Plough Inn Linear ¾ mile or Circular 3 miles

An easy stroll across flat fields to the Plough Inn where you can have a pleasant lunch in a quiet garden accessible with wheelchairs or indoors from the terrace. A moveable ramp is available but it would be advisable to telephone ☎ 01433 650319, the staff are always willing to help.

Route Instructions

1. From the car park return to the road and turn right down to the B6001, turn left and in a few metres turn right down Dore Lane. Walk under the railway bridge and on reaching the entrance to Nether Hall at the bend in the road turn left over the stile by the farmgate, signed "Leadmill Bridge."

2. Follow the farm drive then a path, keeping the fence on your right and crossing stiles, to reach the B6001. Turn right across the river bridge then across the road to The Plough inn.

3. If you would like a stroll along the river cross the bridge and turn right through a stile.

4. Walk as far as the stepping stones, just over 1mile.

5. **To Extend the stroll to a 3 mile circular walk:-**

6. At the stepping stones and footpath post descend down to the river bank to cross the stepping stones over the Derwent River. Climb the bank and turn right to continue following the river, now on the right.

7. In nearly ¼ mile bear left, away from the river, up to a small gate.

8. Pass through the gate and cross the busy A6187 to go over a stile then up a narrow field. Cross the main railway line via two ladder stiles. Walk diagonally right up the next field to go through a fence and hedge gap then on up and through a small gate.

9. Turn right down Jaggers lane. In about ¼ mile join the main road to walk into Hathersage. At the toilets cross the road to walk up the church drive then along a fenced path to the car park.

A very short Linear walk along the Derwent Heritage Way

Directions from Hathersage to Leadmill and The Plough: Turn right out of the car park then left down the B6001. Just after the David Mellor site is the footpath on the left for Derwent Heritage Way. It is a partly surfaced track. You may be able to park just off the road for a drop off. The Plough Inn is a few metres further on up a short hill.

HOPE

Directions

Hope Car Park is off the A6187 Hathersage to Castleton road. As you drive into Hope from Castleton the car park is on the right just before the Woodroffe Arms. There are 2 disabled spaces in the 40 capacity car park and toilets including disabled with your radar key.

Description

Hope stands in the Hope Valley, below Win Hill and Lose Hill, close to the Roman settlement known as Navio.

In the churchyard of the 14th century church of St Peters is the stump of a Saxon cross. This is proof of the age of the village which is recorded in the Domesday Book as one of the earliest centres of Christianity in the area.

The Courtyard Café on the main road opposite the Woodroffe Arms has a flat entrance round the back and space for wheelchairs, The Blue Apple is a very pleasant café just up the Edale Road, unfortunately the interior is not suitable for wheel and pushchairs but there is an outdoor eating area.

Hope & Brough Circular 3 miles

A pleasant stroll across fields and stiles to the village of Brough where you can find refreshment facilities at The Travellers Rest on the A6187. There is disabled parking leading to a flat entrance reached via a small block and slab path. The inn is spacious with a good menu and there are disabled facilities.

Return to Hope via minor roads, fields and the Noe River.

Route Instructions

1. Leave the car park to pass The Woodroffe Arms then turn right down Pinfold Lane. In 250 metres turn left up Eccles Lane and in another 100 metres turn left by the footpath post and bench to cross a stile.

2. Keep straight on passing through the gate/gateway to follow the path round the hillside before bearing right up a wide grass path to go through a gateway.

3. Follow a wood and fence close on the right before crossing a footbridge via two stiles. Keep straight on to cross a ladder stile by the site of the Navio Roman Fort. Bear right down to the road in Brough.

4. Turn left along the road to the A6187, by the Travellers Rest.

5. Turn left and almost immediately right at the pedestrian crossing to walk up Parsons Lane signed "Aston Village only".

6. Follow the road for nearly ½ mile crossing the railway. At Hallum Barn turn left over a stile.

7. Keep straight on crossing three fields and stiles and a footbridge. In the fourth field bear left down to the railway crossing two stiles.

8. Walk down to the road and turn left under the bridge. Stay on this minor road for 400 metres then turn right along the main road for a few metres to cross a stile on the bridge. Descend the steps to follow the River Noe on your left.

9. Pass through gates and stiles to reach the mill via a short flight of steps.

10. Turn right up the track to Killhill Bridge. Turn left to the Edale Road then left again to walk back into Hope along the Edale road passing The Blue Apple Café. At the main road turn right back to the car park.

Ladybower Linear ¾ mile and Circular 3 ½ miles

Directions to Ladybower Reservoir

From Hope drive along the A6187 to the Bamford turn [2 ½ miles]. Turn left at the traffic lights. Follow the A6013 to and through Bamford. In 2 ½ miles at the T-junction with the A57 turn left. In ¾ mile and just after crossing the aqueduct turn right along the reservoir road. In another ¾ mile turn into the Hurst Clough Car Park.

For the linear walk you can either follow the road which would be suitable for a wheelchair and pushchair or:-

1. From Hurst Clough Car Park walk down towards the reservoir and turn right at the T-junction of paths. Follow an undulating path as it winds round the reservoir

first through woodland then open grassland. As you near the viaduct the path ascends to join the road via two gates. EITHER return to the car via the reservoir path or the road OR

2. **For the circular walk** turn right after going through the two gates and almost immediately turn left up the bank to go through a small gate.

3. Keep straight on up the steep field first with a fence on the right then on up the middle of the field to the top right-hand corner. Cross the stile by a gate and continue uphill to go through another gate. Turn right to follow the alternative route through another gate then bear left aiming for the right-hand end of the barn ahead and the waymarked post.

4. Go through small gates crossing a track and still on the alternative route. Walk up the next field to go through a farmgate in the top right-hand corner.

5. Turn right to follow the bridleway route to Rowlee. Go through the gate. Continue on the track which soon veers left away from the wall round Crook Hill following the waymarked posts. As you near a wall and a gate over to the left the bridleway bends round to the right.

6. On reaching the wall ahead go through the gate still following the Rowlee route. Keep straight on up the next two fields going through a small gate.

7. As you reach the brow of the hill at 390 metres [1,279 ft] aim for the left-hand corner of the coniferous wood. Pass through the gate and keep straight on to follow the wood close on the right for nearly ½ mile passing through a small gate.

8. On reaching a farmgate ahead cross the stile or go through the gate on the right.

9. Walk down the path parallel to a wide stony track. [You may need to use the track in some places] In just over ¾ mile you will join the reservoir road by Bridge End Car Park

10. Cross the road and turn left then right down to the reservoir path. Turn right to follow this path. In about ¾ mile the path crosses a branch of the reservoir via steps and between huge pipes, then you will turn right by the waymarked post to walk up the grass path back to the car park at Hurst Clough.

LONGSHAW AND GRINDLEFORD

Directions to the National Trust Car Park at Longshaw Estate

From Castleton take the A6187 to drive back to and through Hope and Hathersage. About 3 miles from Hathersage and having passed Surprise View Car Park, pass The Fox House Inn corner keeping straight on ignoring the Sheffield road to follow the Longshaw Estate National Trust signs to the car park. To reach the Visitor Centre for disabled parking turn right before The Fox House to drive a few metres down the B6521 then bear left through the white estate gates and keep straight on. If you want disabled parking please phone ☎ 01433 637904

To The Grouse Inn by car

Follow the route to The Fox House and Longshaw Estate National Trust Car Park where you keep straight on along the A6187 road for just over ¾ mile. Take the right fork and follow the A625 road south for another 1 mile to The Grouse Inn.

Description

From the Longshaw National Trust Car Park walk down to the visitor centre, this path is suitable for wheelchairs but with a climb back to the car park. The National Trust Visitor Centre and café is open: Weekends Nov-Mar and daily Apr-Oct. The café is all on one level with easy access. The toilets are just beyond the café and the disabled toilets are at the back of the building. There are many National Trust activities centred on Longshaw Estate details of which can be found at the centre.

Sheffield Country Walk Linear

A flat wide walk. [suitable for wheelchairs]

Directions from Hathersage

From Hathersage take the A6187, in about 2 miles you will come to Surprise View Car Park on your left. Here you can stop for an ice cream in the summer and admire the wonderful views before driving a further ¾ mile to a layby on the left opposite the "Hathersage Road Bus Stop", where you can park.

From this lay-by you go through a kissing gate to walk along a flat wide hard packed sandy track with wonderful views across the open moorland to Higger Tor and Carl Wark.

After the walk you can drive on to The Fox House or the Longshaw Visitor Centre and café. [see directions and description]

Longshaw & The Grouse Linear 1 ½ miles

A mainly flat route with one gate for as far as you wish or 1 ½ miles to the Grouse Inn. The inn has a large flat car park with ramps to an outdoor eating area, conservatory and toilets, but no disabled toilets. The views from the inn of the ridges and valleys are well worth a stop at The Grouse Inn.

Route Instructions

From the Longshaw National Trust Car Park walk to the Visitor Centre via a path at the bottom of the parking area. Cross a bridge and follow a path through the trees to the café. From the café walk in front of Longshaw House. Pass through two opposite gates under the conifers to join a wide track. Follow this shale track, going through one small gate, for 1 mile. At the end of the track go through another small gate by the estate gate. Walk down the road to The Grouse Inn.

Grindleford & Padley Circular 3 ¾ miles

A lovely walk through Longshaw Estate and down the shady woodland of Padley Gorge. A wide track will bring you to Grindleford Station where you can have a refreshing drink before a very pretty, steep, rocky and stepped climb up through woods [about 1 in 4]. The return route follows a flat track back to the Visitor Centre. This is the most challenging walk in the book!

Route Instructions

1. Leave the Longshaw Estate National Trust Car Park via a path at the bottom of the parking area. Cross a bridge and turn right. Walk down to the main drive and turn right to follow it to the D6521. Cross the road to go through a gated stile by the white gate to enter The National Trust area.

2. Follow the clear wide path through parkland and at a fork take the left-hand path. Pass through a gate and continue ahead. Cross a stream and turn left down a stone path crossing the stream again before crossing a footbridge over Burbage Brook. Turn left along the Burbage Brook path.

3. At the next footbridge keep straight on by the brook before bearing up right over the rocks and walking towards the woods.

4. After entering the wood go through a small gate. Continue down the rocky path

as you gradually descend the pretty Padley Gorge. At a fork take the right-hand path.

5. As you leave the wood go through a gate.

6. Walk down the rather steep shale driveway and at the T-junction turn left. Continue through Padley to pass the mill, cross Burbage Brook and the main railway line. Immediately after passing the station café turn left before the car parking area.

7. Walk up the surfaced stepped path. Turn left along the pavement for a few metres then cross the road to go over a low stone stile.

8. Climb the steep rough stone stepped route through the woods, with a stream down on the right.

9. After 27 steps bear round to the right, still following the stream on the right. The path is less steep at this point. Soon you will come to an area of large rocks where the path winds on up through the rocks to go through a gate.

10. At a junction of paths, cross a wider path to keep straight on uphill. Cross another path to keep straight on with a small stream on the left.

11. Continue across the open moorland aiming towards a wall over to the left, (this is rather a boggy area). Soon you will reach a stone flagged path which takes you up by the wall to a stile.

12. Cross the stile and walk up to the track where you turn left.

13. Follow the 1 mile track back to the Visitor Centre at Longshaw.

Longshaw & Burbage Moor Circular 3 miles

This is a rugged walk across open access moorland to the north-east of Hathersage, before descending to the Sheffield Country Walk and the softer open woodland of Longshaw Estate. The only climb is up the gradual ascending Sheffield road and the Houndkirk Road, at the start of the route.

The Fox House Inn has a large car park with disabled parking, entrance and toilets, open all year.

Route Instructions

1. From the top of the National Trust Car Park follow the signpost to the "Moorlands Discovery Centre". In a few metres leave the main path to turn right on a narrow path. Walk towards the Fox House Inn. Go through a gate and cross the busy road to the inn.

2. Turn right to walk round the inn passing the car park.

3. Follow the Sheffield road for about ¼ mile then bear off left onto a wide stony

track [Houndkirk Road].

4. Follow the track for about ¾ mile going through a gate. At the gas pipeline signs turn left through a gate. Follow a wide sandy and rocky path with a fence over on the left. Go through a gate on the left.

5. Keep straight on across the heather moorland following a narrow rocky path. Ignore a path off left to continue on down the moor.

6. At a waymarked post and cairns keep straight on downhill. Gradually the path widens out and becomes more grassy.

7. At the junction with a wide track turn left to follow the Sheffield Country Walk track. This point is about ¾ mile from the Houndkirk Road.

8. Walk along the wide flat sandy track for ¾ mile to the main A6187, going through two gates.

9. Cross the road to go through a small gate into the Longshaw Estate.

10. Bear round to the left following the path which shortly meets another path coming in on the right. Continue ahead walking parallel to the road up on your left. Cross a small gated stile onto the road.

11. Turn right and cross the road to enter the drive leading to the visitor centre. Immediately turn left to follow the "Moorlands Discovery Centre" route then the left again up the path to the car park.

Longshaw Estate Circular 2 miles or Linear

An easy mainly flat walk through the open wood and parkland of Longshaw. This is especially beautiful during the spring and early summer when the rhododendrons are in bloom along the path to the lake. The path is of hard shale and sand at the start then rougher and somewhat irregular on a slight decline. After the lake the paths become grassier. The start of the linear route is suitable for wheelchairs.

Route Instructions

1. From the Longshaw Visitor Centre walk along a fenced path in front of Longshaw House to go through one gate.

2. Turn right under the trees to follow a very pretty path through the rhododendrons and across an open stretch to go through a small gate.

3. You are now on a wider but more stony path as you descend slightly to the lake via two more gates. The path bends round to the right on the edge of the lake. [½ mile]

Longshaw Estate with Carl Wark on the horizon

4. Continue round the lake and on along the path through open woodland where you have good views of Carl Wark and Higger Tor over to the right.

5. Go through a gate and in a few metres by the wooden sculpture of an insect turn left.

6. The paths are now more grassy, they may be suitable for pushchairs. Follow a narrow path to go through a gate.

7. Keep straight on along a wider grass path ignoring a path off left. The main path bends round to the right.

8. At a stream and a low insect waymarked sign turn left.

9. Continue up the very gradually ascending grass track for about ¼ mile to a footpath sign.

10. Turn left to follow the track back to Longshaw Visitor Centre. Go through a small gate by the white estate gate and retrace your outward route.

Grindleford Station and The Grouse Circular 2 miles

Directions to Grindleford Station

Leave the Longshaw Car Park to turn left and join the Sheffield road where you keep straight on, passing the Fox House on your right, and immediately turn left down the Grindleford road B6521. In about 1 ½ miles turn right down the station road. Park where convenient.

This walk will give you a shorter route but still with the invigorating woodland climb.

Route Instructions

1. Take a surfaced path between the café car park and the station café.

2. Walk up the surfaced stepped path. Turn left along the pavement for a few metres then cross the road to go over a low stone stile.

3. Climb the steep rough stone stepped route through the woods, with a stream down on the right.

4. After 27 steps bear round to the right, still following the stream on the right. The path is less steep at this point. Soon you will come to an area of large rocks where the path winds on up through the rocks to go through a gate.

5. At a junction of paths, cross a wider path to keep straight on uphill. Cross another path to keep straight on with a small stream on the left.

6. Continue across the open moorland aiming towards a wall over to the left, this is rather a boggy area but soon you will reach a stone flagged path which takes you up by the wall to a stile.

7. Cross the stile and walk up to the track where you turn right.

8. Follow the track to the road via a small gate by the white estate gate.

9. Turn right down the road to The Grouse Inn. [see walk Longshaw and The Grouse for details]

10. Just past the inn cross a stile on the right. Cross three fields passing through a farmgate/gap and two small gates.

11. After the last gate keep straight on through open woodland for a few metres then turn right.

12. If the ground is dry you may be able to walk down a sunken path if not then follow a path to the left of the sunken path.

13. At a junction of paths turn right. Walk on down this wider path going through a gate.

14. At the junction with a minor road turn right down to the main road where you turn right again for a few metres. Turn left at the wall gap to retrace your outward route down the surfaced path to Grindleford Station.

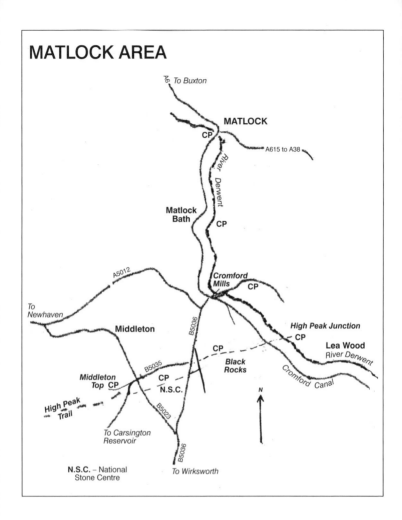

MATLOCK AREA

A6 To Buxton

MATLOCK

CP

A615 to A38

River Derwent

Matlock Bath

CP

A5012

Cromford Mills

CP

To Newhaven

Middleton

B5036

High Peak Junction

CP

Lea Wood
River Derwent

CP

Black Rocks

B5035

CP
N.S.C.

Cromford Canal

Middleton Top CP

High Peak Trail

B5023

N

To Carsington Reservoir

B5036

To Wirksworth

N.S.C. – National Stone Centre

MATLOCK AREA

BLACK ROCKS & STONE CENTRE

Directions

From Matlock take the A6 to Cromford. At the lights turn right onto the A5012 Newhaven road and in a few metres where it turns right keep straight on up the B5036. In ¾ mile turn left at the brown sign for Black Rocks. Follow the minor road, ignoring the first turn off left by the High Peak Trail notice, and then just before the bridge and the 30mph sign turn left at the second HPT notice. Pass a small car parking area on the left and the toilet block [+disabled toilets] on the right to enter the larger pay and display car park. Grid Ref SK 291557 Disabled parking is up to the right as you enter the car park with a picnic area at the side of it.

Directions to The National Stone Centre and Middleton Top by car

If you wish to drive to The National Stone Centre follow the B5036 from Cromford, pass the sign to Black Rocks and in about 1 mile from the traffic lights in Cromford turn right to follow the B5035. The signs to the Stone Centre are clear and give a lot of information. When you reach the car park drive down to the bottom then bear left under the bridge to the disabled area by the centre.

To drive to Middleton Top from the Stone Centre return to the B5035 and turn left. In about ½ mile keep straight on at the crossroads in Middleton. Continue up the B5035 passing "The Rising Sun" on the right and just after the bridge over the road turn right up the minor road to Middleton Top Car Park. [Pay and display]

Description

Although this area is not in the Peak District it is full of interest, variety and history with wonderful far reaching views. The Steeple Grange Light Railway [open at weekends in Jul, Aug and Sep – for more details go to www.steeplegrange.co.uk or read the notices along the trail,] The Stone Centre, Middleton Top Visitor Centre and mainly flat trail walks all add to the interest of this area.

High Peak Junction Linear 1 ½ miles

A walk down the High Peak Trail to High Peak Junction, where there are disabled facilities, an Information Centre with toilets and a picnic area. The wide trail is of hard packed stone and grit. The slope down is very steep so you may wish to go only as far as the winding station.

Route Instructions

From the top car park at Black Rocks walk to the far end by the DCC Countryside notice board, to go through a gateway. Turn left. Before the descent you will see the old engine house and seats that give you wonderful views across the valley. Wheelchair users could return to the car park from this point.

The pick up point is at High Peak Junction. To reach this car park see the Cromford venue page 83.

The National Stone Centre and Middleton Top Linear ½ mile to 1 mile

From Black Rocks Car Park is a flat linear stroll to the Stone Centre and just over 1 mile to Middleton Top which includes an incline of 1in 8 ¼ . There are disabled facilities, a visitor centre with snacks [open at weekends] and a pleasant picnic area at Middleton Top.

If you need more substantial meal than the snacks provided at Middleton Top "The Rising Sun" in Middleton village is a suitable venue. They have a large car park and can provide ramps into the inn and toilets.

Route Instructions

1. From the disabled parking area follow a short path to reach the trail via a wall gap and turn right.

2. Follow the wide flat hard packed surfaced trail. Pass the Steeple Grange Lt. Railway and the first sign to The National Stone Centre.

3. At the second sign to the Stone Centre [which is on the right], turn right to leave the trail via a gate.

4. Walk across the car park then under the bridge to walk down to the Stone Centre.

5. The National Stone Centre has Activities, Special Events, Educational Services, Indoor Exhibition and Rock Detective, also a small café serving drinks and cakes only in the winter, and light meals at weekends in the summer. There are

disabled facilities.

6. To walk to Middleton Top retrace your steps back to the trail and turn right.

7. This is a pleasant stretch with views of the towering limestone cliffs. It is flat as far as the two notices explaining the Wheel Pit and the Incline.

8. Start the 1 in 8 ¼ incline climb to Middleton Top: just over ¼ mile.

9. As you near the top there is a path on the left that will go to "The Rising Sun Inn".

10. Go through a gate to pass the Engine winding building, the Visitor Centre and car park.

CROMFORD

Directions

From Matlock take the A6 south through Matlock Bath. At the crossroads and traffic lights in Cromford turn left to Arkwright Mills. There are two car parks:-

1. Arkwright Mills. In about 300 metres turn left into the mill car park Grid Ref SK299570. Free for blue badge holders.

2. Cromford Canal and Wharf. Pass the entrance to the mills and almost immediately turn right into the car park. There are toilets and free parking for blue badge holders.

Description

The Cromford Canal Car Park has disabled facilities, an easy café and gift shop entrance. There are a greater range of shops at the mill complex with disabled parking and toilets, the museum and conducted tours, as well as gift shops and a café. Richard Arkwright built the first successful water mill here in 1771. The building at Cromford is now part of the Derwent Valley Mills World Heritage Site. After building the cotton mill, Arkwright also built cottages for the workers, a corn mill and the Greyhound Hotel.

There are a number of leaflet guides to be had.

The walks are relatively easy, quietly beautiful and with a glimpse into the early industrial development of the area, which was of great significance locally and nationally.

High Peak Trail Circular 3 miles

The route takes you along the canal towpath before the steep climb up the wooded High Peak Trail, and then a minor road descends to Cromford Mill.

Route Instructions

1. From the mill complex turn left out of the car park and in a few metres cross the road to Cromford Canal Car Park.
2. Join the canal path to follow the pretty route by the canal on your right. In just over a mile you will reach High Peak Junction.
3. Cross the canal and turn right to walk behind the Information Centre passing the old rolling stock before climbing the rather steep High Peak Trail for about ½ mile.
4. At the footpath post, before you reach the top of the incline, leave the trail to turn left. Follow the woodland path round and down to a footpath sign. Take the left-hand route signed "Cromford"
5. Walk under The High Peak Trail to follow a track [Intake Lane] downhill keeping a fence and an old wall close on the right. This is part of the Derwent Valley Heritage Way.
6. In about ¼ mile the track becomes a minor road which leads down to the A6.
7. Cross the busy A6 to go through a wall gap. Turn right to follow a wooded walled path as it winds down to a small car park opposite the mills.
8. Cross the road to enter the Arkwright Mills complex and car park.

Cromford Canal Linear 1 ¼ miles

A flat sometimes narrow towpath walk to High Peak Junction. There are seats along the way and you may see voles as well as water birds.

We think the canal path is not suitable for larger wheelchairs.

It is often used by parents with pushchairs and small children with tricycles.

Route Instructions from Cromford Canal Car Park

1. From the main car park walk up a smooth short path to the canal and turn left.
2. Follow the clear tree-lined towpath with the canal on your right.
3. At High Peak Junction you can buy snacks at the information centre and there is also a picnic area and toilets + disabled toilets.
4. Return on the same route.

Route Instructions from High Peak Junction Car Park

Directions to High Peak Junction Car Park

Turn left out of the Arkwright Mill Car Park or right from the Cromford Canal Car Park. Follow the road over the river and under the railway. In about 1 ½ miles turn right into the free High Peak Junction Car Park.

To reach the canal and Visitor Centre from the car park walk from the disabled parking space up to the metal gate and turn left along a path [indicated for wheelchairs but only when dry!]. Turn right along a surfaced path to cross the river then on up a surfaced track to cross the railway and the canal.

The towpath with the canal on your left is wider and firmer as far as the sheds. Here there are picnic areas.

Lea Wood Circular ¾ mile

A flat pretty walk through very pleasant woodland from High Peak Junction.

Route Instructions

1. Follow the paths across the river and railway from High Peak Junction Car Park. [see Cromford Canal linear walk]
2. Turn left along the canal towpath with the canal on your right.
3. In just over ¼ mile at a footbridge turn left leaving the canal and passing an old house on the right.
4. Follow the clear flat woodland path crossing a bridge over the railway.
5. Soon you will pass Wharf Cottage and then you turn left off the track.
6. Follow a walled path to another track.
7. Turn left to the road then left along the road.
8. In a few metres turn left to follow the path back to the car park.

MATLOCK BATH

Directions

From Matlock drive south to Matlock Bath. At the sharp right-hand bend turn left into the Station Car Park where there is disabled parking. If you wish to use the cable car follow the signs from the car park.

Description

This popular centre in the Derwent Valley is often called Little Switzerland. Warm Springs were discovered here in 1698. John Smedley built the Hydro in Matlock in 1853, now the Derbyshire County Council offices. He also built Riber Castle which overlooks the valley.

Riverside Walk Circular 1 mile

A stroll along hard packed and tarmac surfaces through the gardens on the east bank of the river is very pleasant and suitable for everyone.

Route Instructions

1. From the car park return to the A6 and turn left.
2. Pass "The Midland" and immediately turn left down to the clock pavilion where there are disabled toilets with the radar key.
3. Turn right to walk through the gardens on a tarmac surface and where there are seats. Soon the path joins the A6.
4. Walk along the wide pavement for a few metres before crossing the wide surfaced bridge [slightly humpbacked].
5. Turn right to follow the flat wide surfaced path passing the children's play area, seats, and a shelter.
6. Cross the next bridge to the gardens on the other side of the river and turn right. Here there are seats, a play area, the band stand and information boards.
7. Follow the riverside path back towards the "Peak District Mining Centre and Information" [a large domed pink building]. Pass it on your left.
8. As you near the road by a parking area there is a kiosk serving snacks that is open all year.
9. Pass the kiosk to walk down a block paved slope to pass the circular "Riverside Fish & Chips" restaurant.
10. Follow your outward route back to the car park.

TIDESWELL AREA

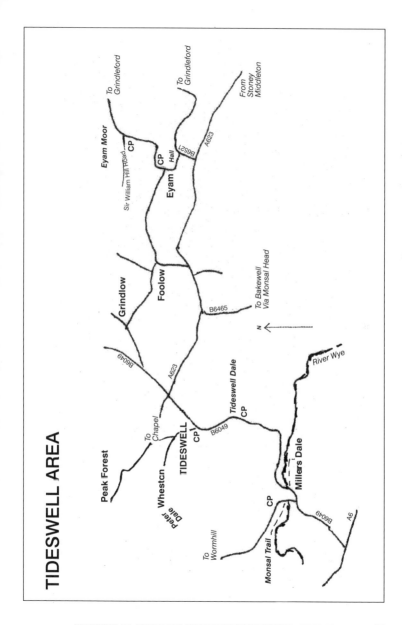

TIDESWELL AREA

EYAM

Directions

From the centre of Tideswell take the B6049 north out of the village. At the junction with the A623 turn right. Follow this road for 2 ½ miles. Turn left up the B6521 to Eyam. As you enter the village turn left and left again. Drive through the village passing the church and Eyam Hall on the right. Turn right up Hawkhill Road to the pay-and-display car park with toilets + disabled toilets; there is another car park a few metres further on which is free but with a request for donations, when we researched this area.

Description

Eyam is known as the Plague village. It is reputed that a travelling tailor inadvertently introduced the plague in a parcel of flea-infested cloth from London. William Mompesson, the rector at the time, persuaded the villagers to stay thus sealing off the village. The plague lasted 16 months and killed 259 villagers. There is a footpath at the back of the church which leads to Mompessons Well where food was left by neighbouring villagers and money left by the people of Eyam who disinfected the coins in vinegar.

Eyam has much to offer: Eyam Hall and Craft Centre, with disabled toilets, craft outlets and a café, where we have used a wheelchair. There is also the church and many plaques on houses describing the history. There is a very good museum and several tea rooms and inns. The well dressings (held on the last Saturday in August) all add to the interest of the village.

Eyam to Foolow Circular 4 miles

A relatively easy walk along tracks and across fields with stiles and gates.

Route Instructions

1. From the car park in Eyam turn left down the road and at the T-junction turn right.
2. Walk up the main village road for about 300 metres. At a fork of roads bear left up Tideswell Lane.

3. Follow this undulating lane, which is surfaced at the start, for 1 ¼ miles, ignoring all tracks off.

4. Up at the junction with the road turn right towards Foolow. Follow this road, ignoring a turn off left, for about ½ mile. Turn right along the Eyam and Grindleford road.

5. The Bulls Head in Foolow, closed on Mondays, is a good halfway refreshment stop. On Tuesdays they offer senior citizen reductions on meals.

6. To continue the walk from the inn turn left down the Eyam Grindleford road.

7. In about 200 metres turn right at the footpath sign and bear left towards a small ruin.

8. Go through a gate, across a grassy track, a broken wall and another small gate.

9. Follow a wall on the right across four fields and stiles. In the fifth field cross a small steep valley and go through a gate.

10. At the top of the next field bear left to cross a broken wall then a small gate. Walk across the hummocky field to go through a gate.

11. Keep straight on crossing a broken wall. You now have a wall on the right. Cross a track via a gate and a stile.

12. Continue ahead crossing 3 fields, 2 stiles and a gate. Follow the wall to go through a gap/gateway on the left, you now have the wall on the right. Cross a stile in the field corner.

13. Keep straight on across 3 more fields via 2 gates to enter a walled and hedged path leading down to the road.

14. Cross the road, the field and the track to follow paths between the houses and across minor roads to reach the top of New Close Road. Keep straight on down and up this road to join the main village road.

15. Turn left opposite Eyam Hall Craft Centre and in about 200 metres turn up Hawkshill Road back to the car parks.

Eyam Moor Circular 4 miles

A stimulating moorland walk with wonderful views. The walking across the moors and down in the Bretton Valley is enjoyable at any time of the year. There are a number of stiles and a steady climb up from Stoke Ford [a pleasant picnic spot by the stream]. The return stretch along the eastern edge of Eyam Moor follows a gently climbing path through the bracken.

Directions to the start of the walk
at the end of the Sir William Hill track

Turn right from the car park in Eyam. Follow this winding road uphill passing Mompesson's Well [where you can stop for a while]. Where the road turns sharp right at the edge of the moorland turn left to park the car at the side of the track.

Route Instructions

1. From the junction of the track and the road cross the stile onto the moors at the "Public Footpath via Stoke Ford to Abney No. 78" sign.

2. Follow the moorland path keeping the wall on your right and ignoring paths off left. After about 30 minutes walking the path bears away from the wall. At a junction of paths and a wall ahead turn right. Cross a wall stile by a gate.

3. Turn right down the grass path above Bretton Brook keeping a wall close on the right. Cross a high wall stile and keep straight on. Soon the wide grass path bears left away from the wall to descend on a narrowing path down into the valley of Bretton Brook.

4. At a junction of paths keep straight on down for a few metres to a T-junction of paths and turn right. Bretton Brook is down on the left.

5. When you reach Stoke Ford Bridge down to the left bear off right, away from the bridge to climb the path up under the trees. The path soon comes out onto the moors.

6. Continue along the well walked path. Cross a stream and a stile then follow a fence on the left. As you start to descend the moors the path widens out into a track where you cross a stile by a gate. At the end of this track keep straight on to cross a footbridge and a stile ahead.

7. Follow the narrow woodland path keeping the stream on the left. Cross a stile to leave the woods.

8. Continue ahead with a wall on the left. Pass through gateways and gates to reach Top Farm.

9. Turn right up the farm drive to the road. Turn right to continue with the walk.

10. Follow the steep road uphill for about 300 metres then round a sharp right-hand bend, after another 500 metres and opposite a large stone barn turn right over a wall stile.

11. Turn left up under the trees, then follow the bracken and heather path up over Eyam moor for about 1 mile, the last part of which has a fence on the left. Go through the small gate to return to the car.

Foolow Circular 2 miles

Crossing fields via some high stiles and a track and minor road.

Directions to Foolow from Eyam

Drive through Eyam ignoring the turn to the car parks. Follow this secondary road for 1 ½ miles. In Foolow park where convenient.

Route Instructions

1. From wherever you park return to the Bulls Head and take the right-hand fork south on the "Wardlow and Middleton" road. Follow this road for nearly ½ mile.

2. At a fork of roads take the right-hand road and almost immediately turn right onto Brosterfield Farm drive. Follow this tarmac drive which leads into a track by the farm. In a few metres and having gone through a gateway turn sharp left to cross a stile.

3. Turn right to walk in a westerly direction crossing 8 fields and 8 stiles and following a wall on the right except in the fourth field where the wall is some metres up to the right.

4. On reaching the track by Stanley House turn right to pass the house on your right.

5. Follow the track and where it turns left keep straight on down for a few metres to cross a stile on the left.

6. Bear right up the field to go through a small gate. Keep straight on up the next field to cross a squeeze stile. Continue in the same direction following field paths crossing, a track via 2 stiles, 3 fields and 2 more stiles. In the fourth field bear very slightly left to walk uphill aiming for the top right-hand corner to cross the stile.

7. Cross the middle of the next 3 fields and stiles. After passing through a gate turn right towards Foolow.

8. Go through a farmgate, cross a courtyard and then on along a narrow gravel path which leads back to the village pond in Foolow.

TIDESWELL

Directions

There is a small car park in the centre of Tideswell. Grid Ref SK151756 As you approach the village from the south on the B6049 it is on the left just after the Horse & Jockey Inn.

Description

The 14th century parish church known as "The Cathedral of the Peak" is a magnificent building. The patronal festival with well dressings, and a week of festivities ending in a torchlight procession with Morris dancing is unique to Tideswell. This is held at the end of June. It was a prosperous market town but no longer sells cattle. Local crafts and produce are sold at the market twice a year. Stone crosses were erected on all roads leading into Tideswell; they were probably resting places for coffin bearers from outlying hamlets and farms. One of these, possibly the best in Derbyshire can be seen in Wheston just beyond the hall.

Tideswell Dale Linear nearly 2 miles

Directions to Tideswell Dale Car Park

Drive south on the B6049 out of Tideswell and in about ¾ mile turn left into the car park. There is disabled parking and toilets and a picnic area. The start of the dale is along a flat hard surface suitable for wheelchairs.

The route down Tideswell Dale is very pretty with seats and a small stream.

Route Instructions

Walk south down the dale for as far as you wish.

To extend the route turn right at the bottom of the dale. Follow a minor road for 1 mile to Miller's Dale. The Anglers Rest ☎ 01298 871323 in Miller's Dale is a welcome refreshment stop at the end of the walk. There is parking for customers. The inn is reached via steps.

Directions to The Anglers Rest by car

From Tideswell Car Park drive south on the B6049 and in just over 1 mile opposite a chapel turn very sharply left back on yourself, signed "Litton Mill". The inn is a few metres on the left.

Wheston & Peter Dale Circular 3 miles

Directions to Wheston from Tideswell Village Car Park

Turn left and in about 100 metres leave the main road at a sharp right-hand bend to keep straight on up a minor road which bends round to the left passing the Market Square on the right. Almost immediately turn left signed "Wheston". Drive up the steep narrow road and in about 1 mile enter the hamlet of Wheston. Just past the minor road to Peak Forest on the right and the Hall on the left is a small layby on the right.

Peter Dale is a lovely limestone dale in the spring when many of the flowers are in bloom especially the orchids. In late summer and autumn the dale can be overgrown and muddy. The route takes you along tracks and minor roads with a descent to the dale and a steep ascent out of the dale.

Route Instructions

1. Start the walk at the layby opposite the farm.
2. Follow the descending minor road for ½ mile. At the bottom of the hill, where paths cross the road, turn left signed "Miller's Dale".
3. Walk down through the varied scenery of Peter Dale. After nearly 1 mile pass the Monks Dale notice board and shortly afterwards you will cross the stile onto the road.
4. Turn left up the steeply winding minor road for about ½ mile.
5. At the road and track junction turn left following the "Pennine Bridleway".
6. In just over ¼ mile keep straight on where the minor road bends right, still on the "PBW". In another ¼ mile you will reach Wheston and return to the car.

Miller's Dale Linear

Directions to Miller's Dale and Monsal Trail Car Park

From Tideswell drive south on the B6049 and continue past Tideswell Dale Car Park. Drive into Miller's Dale and just as you leave the village turn right up Wormhill Road. Almost immediately after passing under 2 bridges turn left into Monsal Trail Car Park. There are full toilet facilities, picnic tables and wheelchairs should be able to manage the trail as far as you wish.

The Monsal Trail tunnels are being opened up and the first phase was completed in 2011. You can now walk from the car park to Wye Dale passing through the tunnels, the longest of which is well lit. It is about 2 miles.

Peak Forest & Dam Dale Circular 4 miles

Directions to Peak Forest from Tideswell

Drive north through and out of the village, passing the church on the left, on the B6049. At the junction with the A623 turn left. Follow this road for 3 ½ miles. In Peak Forest turn right at the traffic lights. Park where convenient as there is no official parking. The walk starts at The Devonshire Arms, where you can only park for refreshments. The car park and inn is all on one level.

The route follows dale/field paths with stiles and gate, a gently climbing track and minor roads.

Route Instructions

1. From the Devonshire Arms cross the road to walk down Damside Lane passing the church on your right [at one time known as the Gretna Green of the Peak].
2. Walk through Damside Farm and before the house in the dale ahead of you turn left to cross the old dam keeping a fence on the left. Turn right signed "Dam Dale."
3. Cross a wall stile and walk behind a house. Continue ahead keeping a wall down on the right before veering away from it, then down towards it again to cross a wall stile. You will now be following the "Public Footpath Miller's Dale" route.
4. Walk behind the extensive barns of Dam Dale Farm then follow a wall close on the right.
5. Walk down the grassy Dam Dale crossing four broken walls and six wall stiles.
6. After the sixth stile turn left up the wide track of the Limestone Way. After about ½ mile at the road junction turn left along the minor road for another ½ mile to the busy A623.
7. Cross the road and turn left. In 100 metres turn right through the waymarked gate. Now follow the wide walled mainly grass track of the Limestone Way for just under ½ mile, going through a farmgate. At the end of the track go through a small gate on the left to join Old Dam Lane.
8. Turn left along the lane to Old Dam for ¾ mile. At the grass island turn left down Church Lane back to the car.

OTHER WALKS/OUTINGS WITH WHEELCHAIR AND PUSHCHAIR FACILITIES

BARTON TURNS MARINA

Situated off the A38 south of Burton-upon-Trent. Drive south from Derby to the Barton-under-Needwood turn. Follow the signs for Barton as you cross the A38 ignoring all signs to Branston Water Park. Just after passing the local sign for Barton-under-Needwood turn left at the small sign for Barton Turns Marina [this is the first sign for this site!] The marina is on the right. Drive up towards the buildings.

This is a very attractive and well laid out site by the canal. All the walkways are flat and surfaced; the entrances to all the shops, cafés, inn and gallery are wide and on one level. The shops include high class butchers and grocers, dress and gift shops, children's shop, "The Waterfront" inn with a varied menu, a delicatessen/café, disabled and child facilities on site and in the eating establishments.

There are paths by the lakes with opportunities for short walks suitable for wheelchairs and pushchairs.

CARSINGTON RESERVOIR

Situated off the B5035 Wirksworth to Ashbourne road and to the south of Carsington village. This site has much to offer boating, cycling, fishing, walking, water sports and wildlife especially bird watching. The Galley café and Mainsail restaurant offer a range of snacks and meals. The "Water Story" exhibition and retail outlets both offer further attractions. Lifts and all toilet facilities are installed. There is plenty of disabled parking and the centre has free wheelchairs and they have two scooters £2.50 per hour to hire. Most of the paths are of hard packed limestone.

The Visitor Centre has a number of leaflets on the activities including three walks, a 1 mile route on a hard surfaced footpath, 3 mile circular route which includes the top of the dam where there are a number of seats and an 8 mile circular walk round the reservoir. There are also linear walks to the Wildlife Centre and the birdhide.

ELVASTON PARK AND CASTLE

Situated off the A6 south of Derby and near the village of Thulston.

Follow the brown signs to the main large flat pay and display car park [about a 10 to 15 minute walk from the castle].

If you are a Blue Badge holder look for the sign to the "Elvaston Cricket Club" which is before the main entrance. It is on the right-hand side of the road just after passing through the village, at the sign turn left. As a badge holder you are authorised to follow this ¾ mile driveway to the disabled and staff car park.

There are a number of walks through the grounds on mainly hard packed wide flat surfaces. The rhododendrons, many stone features and the wildlife make these walks very interesting.

The information centre is open Sat-Sun; the café is open daily in the summer but closed on Mondays in the winter; the toilets + disabled; are all in the cobbled courtyards. There are slabbed paths round the cobbles!

MELBOURNE HALL

To reach Melbourne from Derby take the A514 through Chellaston and go round the A50 island to stay on the A514. In Swarkestone turn sharp left to cross Swarkestone Bridge. Drive up through Stanton-by-Bridge then keep straight on along the B587 to Melbourne. The B587 goes round a sharp right-hand bend. At the next bend leave the B587 to drive down into the town. At the conical bus shelter bear round to the left. The hall and church car park is on the right.

This is a very pleasant walk by the lake on tarmac surfaces. In the courtyard there are craft outlets and a café with easy access. There is a disabled toilet but the access to the small enclosed area is too small for most wheelchairs!

The Cloud Trail is mainly flat and mostly tarmac. Unfortunately the access from Melbourne and Breedon-on-the-Hill are not wheelchair friendly.

Directions to Breedon-on-the-Hill. From Melbourne Hall Car Park turn right to follow the road to Wilson. At the outskirts of the village bear round to the right staying on the main village road. Pass The Bulls Head and go round a sharp left bend. Follow the road to Breedon-on-the-Hill. In about 1 mile at a T-junction turn right, ignoring the first left turn, to drive into the village. At the village green bear round to the left to turn right into Breedon Priory Car Park. There is disabled parking and toilets. The interests include a well stocked garden centre, bookshop, dress and shoe shop, antiques, craft shops and tea rooms.

NATIONAL MEMORIAL ARBORETUM

Situated off the A38 and A513 about 7 miles south of Burton upon Trent.
☎ 01283 792333 www.thenma.org.uk

Open: daily except Christmas Day 9am-5pm.

Extensive disabled facilities: wheelchairs, buggies, "a train", ramps, parking and drop off area and toilets.

Large Visitor Centre with a full café and picnic areas, shop, market place, plants, information of events and a lovely church.

RUDYARD LAKE

If you like sailing/boating, fishing, wildlife, steam trains and easy walking; with some stretches suitable for wheelchairs and pushchairs; no retail outlets and paved areas! then you may enjoy this outing.

From Leek take the A523 Macclesfield road. In nearly 2 miles turn left onto the B5331. In just over ¾ mile and immediately after driving under a bridge turn left up to the Rudyard Lake Station large car park. The café is open from end-Mar to Oct. For the days and times of the steam trains telephone ☎ 01538 306704. From here you can easily walk the ½ mile to the lake along the flat hard surfaced path by the narrow gauge railway. Crossing the dam brings you to the toilets with full facilities including disabled; there is a small Visitor Centre and snack bar with outside seating. The Rudyard Lake Circular Walk is 5 miles on a hard packed undulating path.

STAUNTON HAROLD

Situated off the A514 Melbourne to Ashby road. Drive south from Melbourne and in about 2 ½ miles, having passed the turn to Staunton Harold Reservoir and crossed into Leicestershire, turn right at the brown anvil sign for Staunton Harold Craft Centre and Café. Follow the brown anvil signs. After about 1 mile and a number of bends and junctions turn left at the big "Staunton Estate" sign. Continue up the long drive to the car parks. The Garden Centre has disabled parking.

From the car park there is a short slightly uphill walk along a tarmac drive to the Ferrers Craft Centre and Café. The courtyard is hard brick and paved surface.

The "Staunton Stables" Tea & Luncheon Rooms are open daily throughout the year except Monday's 10–5'ish summer; 4'ish winter; open Bank Holidays. Access is easy and they are well supplied with high chairs. There are disabled toilets approached by a wide brick block passage. Craft, pottery, jewellery, ceramics, baskets etc. are all interesting places to visit.

TITTESWORTH RESERVOIR

Situated 2 ½ miles north of Leek and south of The Roaches off the A53.

From The Roaches return to the A53 and turn right. In about ¾ mile turn right to follow the signs to Tittesworth Water and then the Visitor Centre.

From Leek take the A53 Buxton road and in 2 ½ miles turn left to Meerbrook and Tittesworth Water.

The disabled parking is to the left of the Visitor Centre. There is a very adequate restaurant with good views of the reservoir, outdoor and indoor seating, a well stocked gift shop with a range of walking books.

Two walks are recommended; a 1 ½ mile undulating route suitable for wheel and pushchairs and a 4.7 mile circular walk round the reservoir. A plan of the walks is available from the shop but it does only the main route.

1 ½ mile Part Circular Route

1. From the entrance to the café and shop turn right passing the Blue Badge parking. Just past the walking sign turn left.
2. Follow the main partly surfaced path with good views of The Roaches. Stay on the main path as it bends down and round the valley crossing two footbridges. Continue to follow the red walking signs.
3. At a footpath post turn left on the red route. Walk through the conifer wood. The path turns right over a bridge then right again. You now have a fence on the right.
4. At the next junction of paths turn right again and walk down and up quite a short steep section of the route.
5. At the next footpath sign, which is the same as described in instruction 3, you will bend round to the left to retrace your outward route.

THE NATIONAL TRUST PROPERTIES

Details about these properties, gardens, activities etc can be found in the "Discover Derbyshire" pamphlet available at any of the information and visitor centres. This pamphlet does not give details of disabled and child facilities. If you are a member of the N.T. then comprehensive information can be found in the handbook.

Sites suggested where there are disabled facilities are: Calke Abbey, Hardwick Hall, Kedleston Hall, Sudbury Museum of Childhood.